"I've coached hundreds of CEOs through their toughest moments, and Silver Kung's story captures exactly what separates those who break through from those who break down: an unshakeable belief that there's always a way forward. From rock bottom to Bloomberg's best performing hedge fund, Silver proves that your starting point doesn't determine your destination."

—Mark Moses, founding partner of CEO Coaching International and author of *Make BIG Happen*

"Silver shows us: it always seems impossible—until it's done.

"An incredible journey through the life of a fantastic person never deterred by adversity. Silver enriches his life with a deeper, more fulfilling purpose than pure financial success and recognition. Turning professional success into building a legacy to build a better world for future generations.

"The silver lining is here for all who dedicate their life with passion, integrity, and persistence to reach their dream."

—Benno Kriech, former vice-chairman of UBS Wealth Management

"*Silver Linings* is an honest and heartfelt memoir that captures the author's trials, tribulations, failures, and successes with remarkable openness. Each obstacle becomes a learning experience, making this an inspiring and must-read story of resilience and growth."

—Kavitha Ramachandran, regional chief operating officer of Apex Group

"'Please cherish what you have and be assured that there is always a way forward,' Silver insists, and the power of that promise comes from how hard-won it is. As he stumbles from inherited debt, public shame, and separation from his family into a life he's rebuilt on his own terms, you feel every bruise of his falls and the fragile courage of each decision to stand up differently, not just stand up again."

—Barbara Goodstein, founding and managing partner of R360 Global

SILVER LININGS

FINDING WEALTH, WISDOM, AND REDEMPTION ON THE HARDEST ROAD OF ALL

BY SILVER KUNG

Silver Linings: Finding Wealth, Wisdom, and Redemption on the Hardest Road of All

Published by Worth Books, an imprint of Forefront Books.
Distributed by Simon & Schuster.

Library of Congress Control Number: 2026905641

Print ISBN: 978-1-63763-506-3

E-book ISBN: 978-1-63763-507-0

Cover Design by Bruce Gore, Gore Studio, Inc.
Interior Design by PerfecType, Nashville, TN

Printed in the United States of America

26 27 28 29 30 31 RR4 10 9 8 7 6 5 4 3 2 1

To my wife,

Doriya Li

You were my light when the path was dark,
my strength when I faltered,
and my unwavering companion through
every trial and triumph.

This book—and the life it reflects—
would not exist without you.
With all my love and gratitude,
this is for you.

CONTENTS

FOREWORD

I first met Silver Kung in the Himalayan Mountains.

I had traveled to a spiritual retreat in Rishikesh with my twenty-eight-year-old daughter Amparo, and there we encountered Silver and his wife Doriya. Over the course of a marvelous week together, as we walked ancient paths and sat in contemplation, Silver shared the story of his life. The mountains have a way of stripping away pretense, and what emerged was a tale of such hardship and resilience that I found myself urging him, by the week's end, to put it all in writing.

This book is the result of that encouragement. I am honored that Silver trusted me with his story and honored still to introduce it to you.

As Silver spoke, I thought of Lincoln. In the winter of 1842, a bankrupt Abraham Lincoln wrote to his law partner Joshua Speed that he had become "the most miserable man living." The future liberator of four million enslaved souls and preserver of the American union believed, at that dark hour, that he was destined for failure.

He was wrong, of course, but he could not have known it then. The path from despair to destiny is rarely visible to those walking it.

Here was Silver, a young man who at twenty-seven found himself saddled with ten million dollars in debt he had not incurred, unable to afford baby formula for his infant children, dismissed from teaching positions because his personal misfortune reflected poorly on institutions that prized appearances over character.

In the rigid hierarchy of Taiwanese society, he had been consigned to failure before he had properly begun. His own father believed him to be brain damaged. His classmates abandoned him as though misfortune were contagious.

And yet Silver Kung did not merely survive; he prevailed.

The man who graduated from high school with a 2.7 grade-point average, earning the nickname "Mr. 2.7" that his daughters still tease him about, would go on to found Siegfried Capital, a global asset management firm with just over three billion dollars under management. The student whom no respectable school would admit became a professor, an advisor to sovereign wealth funds, and a citizen of the world whose business acumen has been recognized with Bloomberg's highest honors.

This is, in one sense, a rags-to-riches tale as old as Benjamin Franklin and as enduring as the American Dream itself.

But *Silver Linings* is something more than a success story. It is a meditation on resilience, yes, but more precisely on what the Greeks called *thumos*, that ancient fire in the chest that refuses to be extinguished. Not the mind's decision to persevere. Not the heart's choice to hope. Something older. Something the body knows before the mind can name it.

Thumos is what rises when they tell you what you are not. It is the heat that answers humiliation. It is the part of you that stands when standing makes no sense, that walks when the road offers nothing but more road.

Silver's father called him damaged. His country called him failure. The banks called him debtor. And something in him, something beneath language, said: No. I am not what you have named me. I am what I will become.

That is *thumos*. The spirited refusal to be erased. We made a film about it. Watch it. You will know in two minutes whether this fire lives in you.

Silver's fire carried him across an ocean. From Kaohsiung to Wichita, Kansas, of all places. He went looking for what authoritarian cultures and rigid class systems had denied him: a second chance. The America he found was not perfect, but it was perfectible, and it was open. It rewarded curiosity, creativity, and persistence over mere memorization and compliance.

It valued what a person might become more than what they had been.

The pages that follow contain practical wisdom for anyone seeking to build wealth and navigate the treacherous waters of global finance. Silver writes with refreshing candor about the "boiler rooms" where stock prices were manipulated, about the corruption and familial politics of doing business in Southern Italy, and about the quiet discipline required to spot opportunity where others see only chaos.

His account of building Siegfried on the principle of radical transparency, opening his books completely to any investor who asked, is a rebuke to an industry often shrouded in opacity and self-dealing.

Yet the deeper lessons here are not about finance. They are about character.

Silver Kung is a man who reads voraciously—three to five books and five to seven movies every week—because he understands that knowledge is the one form of capital that cannot be repossessed by creditors or confiscated by governments. He is a man who sits alone at restaurants before opera performances, content in his own company, because he learned early that solitude is not loneliness but rather the crucible in which self-knowledge is forged.

He named his company Siegfried, after the dragon-slayer of Germanic myth, because he knew that the path to victory required confronting monsters.

What you cannot fully glean from these pages, however, is what strikes you immediately upon meeting Silver in person. There is a warmth to him, a ready smile and an open curiosity that puts strangers at ease and turns acquaintances into lifelong friends.

I saw it in those Himalayan evenings. He leans forward when you speak, genuinely interested in your story, your struggles, your ideas. This is not the effect of a man who has forgotten hardship; it is the generosity of spirit that hardship, rightly metabolized, can produce.

Silver's capacity for friendship is extraordinary. He writes movingly of Jennifer Chen in Wichita, of Irene and Annie in New York, of the church members who welcomed a lonely foreign student into their homes. These were not transactional relationships cultivated for advantage. They were bonds of genuine affection that have endured for decades, because Silver understands that wealth without friendship is poverty of another kind.

Most striking of all is his devotion to his family.

The love Silver bears for his wife Doriya radiates through every chapter of this book. She was, as he writes, his light when the path was dark, his strength when he faltered. They held each other and wept watching *The*

Pursuit of Happyness because they knew intimately the desperation Chris Gardner had endured.

Together they climbed out of that darkness, and together they have built a life of meaning and purpose. His daughters Celine and Irene are not merely heirs to his fortune but partners in his philanthropic vision, traveling with him to impoverished villages in the Mekong Delta, learning firsthand that privilege confers responsibility.

Consider the name of the family trust Silver has established: DCIS Capital. The letters stand for Doriya, Celine, Irene, and Silver, in that order.

Most men of considerable achievement would place themselves first. Silver places himself last.

This small detail reveals something essential about his character. The man who was once invisible to his own family, a pariah whose failure was posted publicly for all to see, has built his legacy around the primacy of those he loves. The trust is not a monument to his own success. It is a gift to his wife and daughters, an assurance that they will never know the deprivation and humiliation he endured.

"There is always a way forward," Silver writes, and this simple declaration is the book's animating conviction. It is also, I would suggest, among the most subversive and radical ideas one can hold in an age of cynicism and despair.

To believe in a way forward is to reject the tyranny of circumstance. It is to insist, as Lincoln did after his own season of darkness, that the future remains unwritten.

The greater inheritance Silver leaves is not financial. It is the example of a man who refused to be defined by the cruelties of fate or the failures of others' imagination. It is the demonstration that defeat, rightly understood, is merely prologue. And it is the reminder that success means nothing if it is not shared with those we love and used in service of those who struggle.

"One generation plants the trees," goes the Chinese proverb that Silver cites, "and the next enjoys the shade."

You are reading in the shade right now.

Silver planted this. Page by page, memory by memory, he put his hands in the dirt of his own humiliation and made something grow. Not for himself. He already knows what he survived. He carries it in his body, in the way he puts his name last, in the way he leans toward you when you speak.

No. He planted this for you.

You, who have been told what you are not. You, who have swallowed the verdict of small men in small rooms. You, whose name has been synonymous with someone else's disappointment.

This shade is yours now.

Rest in it. Feel how it cools the burning. Let it remind you that someone walked the sun-scorched road before you—and lived.

But do not stay here.

Shade is not a destination. Shade is a gathering of strength. Shade is where you sit until you remember that you, too, have seeds in your pocket. You have been carrying them all along, waiting for permission you never needed.

Here is what Silver is telling you, if you listen:

Your story is not their story of you.

Your story is a tree that does not exist yet. It is waiting in your hands, in your choices, in the first terrifying step you have not taken.

Plant it.

Plant it in the rocky soil they said would never hold you. Plant it in the silence where your name should have been spoken with pride. Plant it in the ground you will claim as your own, that you will call, at last, home.

One generation plants. The next enjoys the shade.

And then—because this is how it has always worked, because this is the only thing that has ever mattered—*they plant again.*

Charlie Garcia
Founder, R360 Global

INVITATION

Even When Times Are Tough, There's Always a Way Forward

Our greatest glory is not in never falling,
but in rising every time we fall.

—Confucius' philosophy

No one's life is easy all the time. No family is untouched by challenges. It does not matter what country you are from, your ethnicity, or what religion you practice—pain is part of the human condition. Even those born into privilege and affluence, and those who achieve it on their own, face obstacles and experience tragedy. Whether it comes in the form of financial, physical, or emotional pain, everyone must endure times of difficulty and uncertainty. But it is also true that everyone can experience joy and success!

My story is one of endurance and resilience. It is also about hope and love. It is for anyone, regardless of background, who seeks a way forward—a way to overcome hardship and live a meaningful, happy life. For my family members, friends, and all who honor me simply by reading this book, I hope to provide an example of how life can indeed be beautiful.

I was born in Taiwan and educated in the US and, later, China. Although I now run a global fund management center with around $3.1 billion in holdings, I started with less than nothing; I began my career as a twenty-four-year-old with massive debt totaling over $10 million. I was unable even to afford baby formula for my two infants.

As I share stories about my life and offer the lessons I have learned, I hope you find something of yourself in these pages, and something you can apply to your own pursuit of happiness and prosperity. I especially hope this book inspires you to brush off your knees and stand up tall after those times when you've fallen.

Please cherish what you have and be assured that there is *always* a way forward.

1

How I Started Out Minus $10 Million

In 1996, when I was only twenty-four years old, I had my name signed to a life-changing document. I didn't know the details of this agreement at the time, but it turns out I was guaranteeing a $15 million Taiwanese bank loan to assist my father's business. It is a frequent practice in Taiwan for one's children, especially the eldest son, to be a loan co-guarantor. The idea, from the bank's perspective, is that by pledging your son's future, you would be incentivized to do everything in your power to repay the debt. Traditionally, adult children in Taiwan are also obligated to support their elderly parents. Taiwanese children are responsible for the "sins" of their fathers, and the banks do not mess around; they protect their balance sheets above all. One effective way to do so is to hold your family hostage.

Still, I didn't give this contract a second thought, and I certainly didn't anticipate the consequences of the deal my father had made. I continued living my life, feeling unencumbered and committed to furthering my education and career.

By 1997, I was living in New York, studying to earn my master's degree in Investment Management at Pace University. Before that, I had earned a bachelor's in aerospace engineering at Wichita State University and was excited about pursuing a career in finance. I had every reason to believe that my father's business in Taiwan was going well. He had started with a brilliant idea: manufacturing and selling electric scooters. This, of course, was long before Elon Musk entered the picture. There was a clear demand for electric vehicles in Taiwan, where approximately twenty-three million people live, and twelve million gas-powered scooters exist. There are many reasons why but, indeed, it is a preferred way of commute for most people in Taiwan even today. The traffic and air pollution are terrible there, and my father wanted to help alleviate the effects of climate change.

In fact, my father chose an opportune time to start his business, because in 1996, Taiwan's governing Nationalist Kuomintang Party (KMT) was actively incentivizing companies to address the issue of reduction of global-warming gases.

Initially, people resisted buying electric scooters because the new technology involved made them quite expensive—almost twice the cost of gas-powered scooters. That's when the government's environmental bureau subsidized the purchase of electric scooters, making them affordable for significantly more people.

This government support was across all departments. It included tax cuts from the Treasury, architectural regulations from the Ministry of the Interior that forced new buildings to install charging ports, and further provisions from the environmental agencies supporting other clean-energy vehicles besides electric scooters. This planned government program was intended to have an eight-year incubation period.

Thus, not only was my father's business receiving government support; consumers were also given government incentives to buy his company's product. It was a win-win-win for Taiwan, its citizens, and my family. It also was a win for the environment.

My father's company boomed, and by 1999, just three years after establishing the business, he was working on an initial public offering (IPO). He put everything he had into it, mortgaging his homes and land—and his son's future!

After I graduated from Pace in 1999, I moved back to Taiwan to pursue a career in finance. I soon took a job at an investment bank in Taipei and worked on IPOs for its clients. I decided to quit that job the following year because another company had acquired the firm, and I didn't want to stay in the new company. After some contemplation, I moved back to my hometown to help my father's company. It made sense for me to work with him, given my expertise in bringing companies to market with IPOs.

In 2000, however, everything changed. The Democratic Progressive Party (DPP) took power and immediately reversed all of the KMT's policies. They refused to honor the previous government's promises, revoking all the subsidies and support once offered to environmentally conscious businesses and consumers. It was devastating for many, including my family. My father's once-thriving company collapsed overnight, and we were inundated with calls from creditors and investors.

I still vividly remember that night. We were all watching the evening news together when we saw the new head of Taiwan Environmental Protection Administration (EPA) say that he would revoke all support for electric scooters. We were stunned into silence—absolutely speechless. If the government wished to revoke an established national major development plan that was passed at the Executive Yuan, it should have gone through all the necessary procedures, including hearings and meetings, before taking such action. But that's not what the head of the EPA did. He just spoke his plan out loud on the TV. The very next day, creditors and investors came to the office and requested that

Dad's company return their monies. It was like a running squeeze.

The company's business plan was based on the government's promised incubation period. Now, only five years into that eight-year incubation, support—and thus sales—instantly evaporated. The new factories still under construction were scrapped. It was all a terrible waste.

The bank went after me for over $10 million because it couldn't recoup its money from the business.

Taiwan had no real bankruptcy protection. There was just the personal guarantee, in my case, from the eldest son. By then, I was twenty-seven and raising a family. Imagine my shock when my personal balance sheet dropped to negative $10 million!

I started teaching finance at various universities, but the bank had court orders to deduct one-third from whatever monies I was paid. A professor's salary—particularly a part-time professor's—is pitifully low. It was evident that with an income of only two-thirds that salary, I could never afford to pay off my debt. To make matters worse, I was not rehired when the semester ended.

The dean of the finance department at one university called me into his office to personally fire me. The school reasoned that my employment reflected poorly on them; it was a bad example for students to have a finance professor who couldn't manage his own money. This scenario was repeated several times. I could no longer obtain a teaching position except for at one school—National

Kaohsiung University of Science and Technology—for which I am eternally grateful. Aside from that institution, the door to teaching was mostly closed. I also consulted for some companies on and off for about two years; all the while, the government was garnishing those earnings too.

Surprisingly, I was not angry or upset. All my brain power and energy were focused on surviving. I was desperate to find ways to feed my family their next meal; we couldn't even afford basic necessities. It is an understatement to say that we were poor. In fact, many years later when my wife and I watched the movie *The Pursuit of Happyness*, featuring Will Smith, we held each other closely and cried so hard as the film credits rolled because we knew exactly what Chris Gardner, the real-life person whom Will's character was based on, had been through as he struggled to overcome homelessness and poverty while also caring for a young son.

With only ten US dollars in my pocket, I wracked my brain to figure out how to make it through the month. I had put down a $100 security deposit for borrowing privileges at the National Sun Yat-Sen University Library, so I went there to get my money back. The librarian gave me multiple forms to fill out, saying my money would be refunded in one month. I ultimately said, "No thank you," because I couldn't wait another month.

What's more, the deposit wasn't worth sacrificing my commitment to reading library books. I prize learning and still use most of my free time to read. Learning has intrinsic value because it opens opportunities and expands one's worldview. I would figure out another way to earn money.

My father had a very hard time, and, in effect, the failure of his business cost him his life. He was only fifty-eight years old when the change in government policy was announced. Three months prior, he had received a clean bill of health at his annual medical checkup. Then, only three months after the announcement, he began having trouble breathing. When he went to the doctor again, he was diagnosed with stage 4 lung cancer and died a few months later.

It was a very dark time for my family. Fortunately, my mother was a retired elementary school teacher and could get by on her pension. I, on the other hand, was on the hook for $10 million and had a family to care for. So, in 2003, I moved to Hong Kong to work for a Taiwanese asset management business. Investment banking was a perfect match for my skill set, and, as a consultant, I didn't have to put up capital. But, most important, the Taiwanese government could not take a third of my earnings.

Furthermore, my record was clean. The collection matter in Taiwan was civil, so I was not a criminal. I had received my first credit card in Hong Kong and set up a bank account. Once I was settled there, I had no obligation to pay off my inherited debt. I started a new life and a new career. I was free!

However, there was a significant trade-off: Yes, I was trying to secure a comfortable future for my family . . . but I had to leave them behind in Taiwan until I earned enough to bring them over.

Thankfully, everything turned out well in the long run. I was doing work I enjoyed and becoming a global citizen. The new company that employed me benefited from China's ascendency in international capital market dealings. They had the platform and the knowledge to do IPOs, bond issuance, and mergers and acquisitions (M&As).

The M&As I worked on presented another trade-off: It is a high-risk, high-reward business wherein "success fees" are the primary form of compensation. I was taking a big gamble by working in this field. In the best-case scenario, a deal goes through, but it takes a year to a year and a half to get paid. In the worst-case scenario, the deal never materializes, nor do the fees. You have wasted all the time you've spent. Thankfully, though, the risk paid off in my case.

During this time, the banks in Taiwan that held my note, sold their nonperforming loans, including mine, to a private equity asset management company at a 70 percent discount, as they just wanted to get some money back to clear their books. When *that* company could not recoup their loans, they sold them to an individual at a deeper discount. This individual was an early venture capitalist who came to me with a proposal: Would you consult with me and help me set up a business? He saw sweat-equity value in me; among other things, I could help vet the many investment proposals he received.

He promised to eventually waive my debt, so over a period of two years I worked part-time for free. He was true to his word, eventually waiving most of my $10 million debt. I was still responsible for the rest—about $1 million—but at least I wasn't worried about how I'd pay for rent and food. I learned the hard way that there is a solution to every problem. Hard work and perseverance pay off.

As you can imagine, these experiences led me to distrust governments and banks everywhere. Since then, I have managed my finances wisely. I have not taken on any other bank debt, and if I charge something on my credit card, I only buy what I can pay off in a month. Even today I have a zero balance on all my credit cards.

I operate my business in a similar way—debt-free. I am conservative about spending money, a financial strategy that has enabled me to build my start-up hedge fund in Hong Kong, which I'll discuss in more depth later in this book.

In the meantime, let me take you to back to my oppressive high school days, when I felt like a failure and an embarrassment to my family—so much so that after graduation, I fled to the US.

2

Kaohsiung Schools: "Mr. 2.7"

Academic achievement and diligent study are extremely prized in East Asian culture. Society considers studiousness a ticket to upward social mobility. There, academic success is earned the hard way: School is rigorous, and expectations are high. Taiwan's primary and secondary school days are typically nine to ten hours long, followed by plenty of homework.

I lived in a small town in the countryside, about one hour from Kaohsiung City. It was a wonderful place to grow up, despite frequent political upheavals and almost weekly earthquakes and typhoons. As children, we would play outdoor games on the farmlands and make our own toys.

However, one significant downside to living in a rural area was that no good secondary schools were nearby. So, after I graduated elementary school, my parents sent me to a boarding school a sixty-minute drive from my home.

The boarding school was a military camp—at least, that's what it felt like. Each class had about fifty students, and the administration maintained quite a rigid schedule: Wake-up was at 6:00 a.m. in a dormitory room with all the other boys; classes were held from 7:00 a.m. until 5:30 p.m.; followed by dinner; then a return to the classroom at 6:30 p.m. for a night study session; and back to the dorm for lights out promptly at 10:30 p.m. The teachers were like army drill sergeants. We repeated this routine day in and day out.

Students were pushed to the limit—study, study, study; memorize, memorize, memorize—and we were constantly supervised. Any score less than perfection, even a 96 out of 100, was punished by a slap on the hands or on the butts with a stick. All classes were strictly academic—there were no art, music, physical education, or enrichment activities.

I was miserable in the prisonlike atmosphere of boarding school. It stripped me of my freedom, including my most cherished freedom: studying subjects that interested me. But I was raised to be obedient. I wasn't taught to think independently, so I just gritted my teeth and did what I was told to do. I didn't know there were plenty of ways to learn enjoyably and live happily. If I had told my parents I hated school, they would have disowned me!

I loved liberal arts, especially history. I would read books on my own about different cultures, warfare, Chinese history, and Ancient Greece, among other topics. I also loved reading novels. But imagine this: I was afraid of getting caught reading for pleasure at home! If I heard my father's footsteps approaching outside my door, I would quickly close my book, hide it, and sit up straight at my desk as if I had been studying the way he expected me to.

Teaching students to think critically and creatively was never the objective of Taiwanese secondary schools back then. Instead, the goal was continued advancement; you were driven to get to the next academic level at the best possible school. You were to earn superior grades in junior high, excel at a superior high school, and graduate from a superior college. This was the societal expectation, the parental expectation, and the peer expectation.

In 1980s Taiwan, you didn't go to a local high school near your home. Instead, the educational system administered an entrance exam when you graduated from junior high and then ranked students based on the results. The highest-scoring students were assigned to the first senior high, and when it was at capacity, the next group was sent to the second senior high, and so on.

Although junior high was a dismal environment where I did not distinguish myself, I somehow qualified for the prestigious Tainan First Senior High. That school proved to be a miserable, authoritarian experience as well.

A child's success in school is a badge of honor for his or her parents, so mine were understandably very proud of me when I was accepted to Tainan First. They thought that meant I was smart. But I felt like a fraud. I wasn't smart—*all* the other students there were brighter than me! I was a complete failure in high school, and my self-esteem suffered big-time.

Still, there were a few rays of sunshine at Tainan First. I was fascinated by my one (and only) year of history class. I also took advantage of extracurricular activities that were unavailable in junior high school, such as the astronomy club. The group met next door to the Chinese chess club. I had never played chess there before, but the other students encouraged me to try, and I beat every one of them!

Winning a chess game was like a victory in the wars that I loved to study. Both chess and warfare require the ability to think many steps ahead of your opponent in ever-changing conditions. Playing chess was also a distraction from my unhappiness, and winning momentarily boosted my self-esteem. I placed first at the chess competitions at Tainan First for two consecutive years.

Another source of unhappiness was my parents' insistence that I study STEM subjects, not liberal arts. High school in Taiwan is only three years; after year one, you must choose one track or the other—and you must study those subjects exclusively. If you wanted to study mathematics, you couldn't study literature, and vice versa. The decision represents a three-year commitment, and it is a tough choice for many sixteen-year-olds to make.

I, of course, had no doubt about my preference for liberal arts. However, the direction of my education wasn't my decision to make; it was my parents'. This scenario is almost unthinkable in the US, where many students enter college without a clue about what they want to study and then change their areas of concentration multiple times—without parental input.

My parents were unwavering; they wanted me to be a doctor, so they demanded that I study subjects preparing me for that path. Because my heart and mind craved liberal arts subjects, we agreed to a small compromise: I would enroll in the STEM track and become an engineer, not a doctor, because a level of creativity, innovation, and design were involved in the engineering curriculum.

Denied the option of studying what I really wanted, I was miserable. And high school was a pressure cooker. In fact, the academic pressure almost literally killed my younger brother—he overdosed on sleeping pills and thanked God he survived when his stomach was pumped. That seemed to be his act of rebellion. Afterward, my parents went easy on him and put even more pressure on me. (I was also the eldest son, so there was a bigger burden on me to begin with.) I didn't rebel by attempting suicide; instead, I rebelled by not studying very hard.

Besides being slotted into a curriculum that didn't suit me, the teaching methods used in the Taiwanese educational system were incompatible with my learning style. They focused on memorizing everything—facts in the textbook, vocabulary, formulas, etc. For example, in English courses, you had to memorize all the grammar, vocabulary, idioms, and so forth; then you were tested as if you have a photographic memory. The exams consisted of entire printed pages of the textbook with blanked-out words, and your job was to fill in the blanks.

I scored the worst grade in my entire English class. But the funny thing is that today, my English ability is probably the best among them!

In my senior year of high school, a new English teacher arrived fresh from graduate school and made a lasting impression on me. Her teaching methods violated the school's norms. Instead of memorization, she surreptitiously taught us English songs and gave us novels to read. But she was an anomaly. My grades in her class weren't great, but she breathed life into the subject and helped me a lot.

The ability to solve problems quickly and regurgitate information automatically—both of which eluded me—were rewarded with good grades. I graduated from high school with a 2.7 grade point average. Later in my life, my daughters, Celine and Irene, nicknamed me "Mr. 2.7" and teased me about my GPA. Both were very anxious about their own grades, but I've always told them not to worry, and I hold myself out as an example of someone who has succeeded despite poor high school grades. In any event, my daughters needn't have worried about their academic performance, as both have excelled in school.

In Taiwanese society, student failure sets off a chain of negative assumptions and reactions: If you don't do well at school, then you are stupid; and if you are stupid, your parents are ashamed of you; and when they are ashamed, they don't want you around. I was invisible to my family and their friends—a pariah—so I felt ashamed and isolated, too.

Even my peers abandoned me, as if academic failure were contagious. The high school contributed to this feeling by posting student names and grades, so my ranking at the bottom of the class was publicized for all to see. The posting was intended to motivate students, but it had the opposite effect on me: It demoralized and demotivated me.

I had made one good friend at the beginning of the school year, and on Sundays, we would go to the library together to study. He worked hard because he wanted to go to a highly ranked college, but I would choose books from the shelves to read for pleasure. Suddenly, my friend stopped talking to me. We no longer spent Sundays together, and he didn't answer my phone calls.

He never said, "Hey, Silver, I think we should both study hard," or "I don't think our friendship is working out." Instead, my once-best friend disappeared from my life, leaving me heartbroken.

My parents' reaction to my poor academic performance was even more devastating. They never told me directly that I embarrassed them. Still, I knew they were ashamed and really didn't want me around. Then one day, I had tangible proof of how they felt: I overheard my father talking to my mother, thinking I was out of earshot. He said he suspected I had some kind of brain damage. The implication was crystal clear—I was stupid and incapable of learning.

After graduating high school, I tried studying at a computer school. When that effort was unsuccessful, I fled Taiwan. I went as far away from home as possible—to the United States.

Why did I choose the US, besides its distance from home? It was common for Taiwanese youth to study abroad, especially in the United States. Taiwan comprises three major cultures: Chinese, Japanese, and American. There was something magical about the US for me. After all the American movies I had seen and books I had read, it seemed my natural destination.

Another point in favor of the US: Thomas Edison was an American. Edison was my idol; he understood how scientific principles could answer human needs and improve our way of life. I had always wanted to be like him. I read many biographies about Edison, Nikola Tesla, and other inventors. Edison loved reading about Western history as much as he loved reading about and experimenting with chemistry. He stirred aspirations in me to become an inventor. After all, one of his creations, the lightbulb, became the universal symbol for a bright idea.

I didn't know how to start the process of applying to American universities, so I went to one of Taiwan's many small consulting companies that help students apply to colleges abroad. An advisor looked at my credentials and concluded that a 2.7 GPA and no SAT or TOEFL (Test of English as a Foreign Language) scores doomed my candidacy. She told me what I already suspected: I didn't have many desirable options.

I took a shot and applied to Wichita State University (WSU), which *Forbes* consistently ranked around 485th among US colleges, with a 95 percent acceptance rate. I was rejected. I wasn't even accepted to a middling school in a small town in the middle of America! That's what bad shape I was in.

The advisor suggested I attend the Intensive English Language Center program offered by Wichita State as a preparatory stepping stone. I attended the language school for six months—four months to study English, followed by two months of academic work. Upon completion of the intensive class of anthropology and a well-written essay, they approved my acceptance to the university.

My hopes were high that Wichita State would give me back my life and my sense of worth. I knew it would have been an entirely different story had I stayed in Taiwan. At long last, I was on the yellow brick road in Kansas, attending university, with sunny skies, colorful rainbows, and a bright future ahead.

3

A Whole New Life: Wichita State University

There is an old Chinese saying, 韜光養晦以待天時, that encourages staying low, building up strength, and waiting for the right time to rise. Attending Wichita State was my time to rise. It represented both a turning point and a highlight of my life—I realized I was exceptionally competent, not stupid. This realization brought with it a rising and sustained confidence, hope, and a passion for lifelong learning.

At WSU, I felt alive and saw endless possibilities. My mind was challenged. I soaked up knowledge like a sponge with infinite capacity. And I loved every minute of it!

When I took calculus in my first year, I achieved the distinction of being the best student in the class. What a change from my poor high school academic performance! I proved my parents wrong; their concern that I was mentally impaired was utterly unfounded. Most importantly, I demonstrated to *myself* that I was capable.

I relished my independence and benefited from my freely chosen lifestyle of relative solitude. For the first time in my life, I was free to study whatever I wanted and go wherever I pleased.

Despite my parents' disappointment in me for my high school failures, at least I was studying in the US for a profession they deemed sufficiently worthy and acceptable: engineering. They gave me $10,000 to cover tuition and living expenses in college. It wasn't nearly enough, but I hesitated to ask for more and learned to live frugally.

Once I was attending classes in the US, I understood why I had done poorly in high school. While I was in Taiwan, the reasons for my academic failure didn't matter—I was just labeled stupid. But the American educational system, unlike the Taiwanese, encourages independent thinking, creativity, risk-taking, experimenting, and collaborating. I loved the analytical and creative processes and became skilled at synthesizing information.

Studying engineering at WSU was rigorous and challenging yet required little to no memorization. Exams did not consist of filling in the blanks on a textbook page like at Tainan First; instead, they involved problem-solving. Many in-class tests were open-book; some allowed you to bring study notes; and others were take-home tests.

When I was first assigned a take-home test for my aerospace engineering course, my professor gave the class a two-week deadline. The assignment instructions consisted of one (deceptively) simple sentence: Design a garbage bin with a volume of 178 cubic feet to be installed in US National Parks. I scoffed at the extended deadline and figured completing it would take two hours, not two weeks.

I was wrong; the assignment took fourteen sleepless days to complete! There were umpteen variables and calculations involved, such as determining the best materials and considering forces like wind that could destabilize the bins.

There is another, somewhat ironic way WSU differed from the generally rigid Taiwanese universities: the early morning punctuality of students to class. My first class in aerospace engineering started at 7:05 a.m. I usually stayed up working in the lab until 3:00 or 4:00 a.m., went back to sleep for two or three hours, and arrived in the classroom at 6:50 a.m. Why? It was an essential course, and all the engineering students arrived early to fight for the front table in the classroom. So, I arrived even earlier to ensure I'd get a seat at that table. By contrast, college students in Taiwan usually moseyed in late for 9:00 a.m. classes. This early morning delayed start was one of the only leniencies, likely because students studied late into the night.

Even though I am not in the engineering field now, the kind of analytical, creative, and logical training I received at WSU is still invaluable. The skills I acquired influence how I conduct business today, whether creating business models, problem-solving, considering variables, or making decisions. I try to offer my daughters the benefit of my experiences, teaching them to think creatively and synthesize information; I encourage them to use computer searches and other sources to discover the underlying framework and then concentrate on solving the larger problem.

• • •

I chose Wichita State for much more than its intensive English language program and, later, its aerospace engineering academic specialty. I looked forward to living in another weather climate, meeting a variety of people, experiencing a new culture, and learning in a Western academic environment. I welcomed these changes and did not have difficulty adjusting because I embraced novelty and adventure (and still do)!

I was excited to escape the heat of Kaohsiung City, where winter temperatures average 78 to 80 degrees, summer is brutal, and earthquakes and typhoons are the norm. Like a kid, I was excited to see and touch snow! I also wanted to go to a place where nobody speaks Chinese so I could learn English and be exposed to Western thinking. The Taiwanese generally form tight social circles, but I wanted to meet a larger, diverse demographic group of acquaintances. Still, I had a few Asian friends at WSU—one Malaysian and one Taiwanese—with whom I still keep in touch.

Wichita's demographics are homogeneous—70 percent of the population is white—yet, as a foreigner, I was greeted with warmth and acceptance. Few people there had traveled to Asia or had even met an Asian (or any other foreigner), so their impressions were limited to misconceptions from American television.

However, people genuinely wanted to learn about me and my culture. I did not experience discrimination based on my accent or the color of my skin; to the contrary, it was as if I assimilated in Wichita.

My first social encounter with foreigners was with people from a local church who welcomed me with open arms. At first, I thought they were just being kind because their religion valued helping strangers, or perhaps they wanted to try to convert me to believe in Jesus. But neither appeared to be their primary motivation. One guy in particular, Chuck, invited me into the community, bringing me to church gatherings and Bible study groups and introducing me to other folks. These were my first relationships with Americans, and I was incredibly grateful for their kindness.

I also met another student at WSU, Jim, may he rest in peace, who was studying electrical engineering. He was ten years older than me, yet he made me feel special . . . and smart! We took some courses together, and I would help *him* with homework. Jim was married to Mary Jo and had two sons, Josh and Jeremiah. I soon became part of their family and we remain close to this day. They were very caring and showed me how things were done in America. We frequently had dinner and celebrated holidays together. Jim would help me move furniture and fix things and was there for me whenever I needed him. These people became my family, and I was grateful for them.

Even though I had made friends and had an "American family," I spent most of my time alone—by choice. I lived in a small apartment on the outskirts of the city and enjoyed my solitude. When I wasn't studying, I read books and watched movies. One Japanese author, Haruki Murakami, had a particularly profound influence on me. He wrote *Hear the Wind Sing*, which depicts with remarkable accuracy the small details of the protagonist's mind and thoughts. I also frequently went to theaters by myself and often stayed for twelve hours straight, watching four or five movies in a row! Later in the book, I will describe other books and movies that influenced me tremendously at various stages of my life.

• • •

Wanderlust is part of my nature, and I traveled all over the Midwest. When I arrived at WSU, I bought a used, beat-up, manual stick from a Taiwanese friend. I later learned it was a raw deal: He had bought the car two weeks prior for $500 and sold it to me for $2,400. Nevertheless, I had my own wheels! I would end up driving three different cars during my time in Kansas and went on road trips that presented me with all kinds of unexpected adventures.

On one extended road trip, the car broke down in the middle of nowhere. Without a cell phone back then, I had no way to call for help. I walked a mile or two before I found a house with a light on. I knocked on the door and was greeted by a man pointing a gun at me. I couldn't blame him—it was 2:00 a.m. in a remote area. Fortunately, he let me come in to call for help.

After a year, I got rid of that car and bought another used car for a couple thousand dollars. It was a decent vehicle, and I drove it for two years—until I flipped it over onto its roof. I was driving up a ramp to the highway on a snowy day, and the roads were icy and slick. The car was totaled but fortunately, I wasn't hurt.

My third used car was much better: a speedy Chevy Camaro sports car. Once, I drove it all over the Midwest, traveling north through Illinois and Wisconsin, and had another mishap. This time, I hit a deer in the middle of the night! Both the car and I were unhurt, but I'm not sure about the deer; he limped off into the woods.

I would frequently drive for four or five hours straight through rural America without a destination in mind. I guess you could say I was looking for surprises. Google Maps and GPS didn't exist then, so the only option for getting directions was to go to AAA and get those huge paper maps with tiny print, which were impossible to fold. Sometimes I wouldn't even bother with a map; I didn't care if I ended up driving in circles. It was just fun to keep moving and wondering, *Am I taking the right road?* I'd have internal debates in my head about which exit to take or turn to make next. It was like doing a jigsaw puzzle without referring to the picture on the box cover.

Once, I drove west on 21st Street from Wichita State without a destination for about an hour or two. I became curious when I arrived at a big hill. I stopped the car and climbed to the top. Lo and behold, I discovered a huge, beautiful lake below. Only later did I learn it is Lake Cheney. I also saw interesting buildings and small farms and talked to the various people I encountered. After I arrived home, I took out the area map and saw the lake featured prominently. If I had read the map in advance, I wouldn't have had the pleasure of being surprised.

Then there was the time I decided to visit a friend who lived in Milwaukee, Wisconsin. I could have easily flown to see her, but instead, I chose to drive the thousand miles for a leisurely twelve hours, enjoying the landscape along the way. I was also inspired to visit particular places by reading about them or seeing them in movies. For example, I really liked the movie *The Bridges of Madison County* (1995) and drove to Des Moines, Iowa, to see the bridges for myself.

Best of all, I loved the solitude. Even though I didn't have many friends, there were some people I could have invited to travel with me. I preferred being alone.

It wasn't a problem to balance my intensive studying with traveling. I would go away during long holiday weekends and winter, spring, and summer breaks. In addition to exploring the US, I traveled to Europe when time permitted. I learned how to spend as little money as possible, sleeping on benches in train stations or paying $5 a night to sleep with a bunch of strangers on the floor in youth hostels. Even if I had wanted a friend to accompany me, which I didn't, not too many people would have wanted to travel on a budget like that.

Once, I slept on an airport bench, washing up in the restroom, and took a bus or tram from terminal to terminal, visiting the shops and scrounging up food like Tom Hanks's character in the movie *The Terminal* (2004).

I was determined to explore the entire world. At one point, my family was gathering (I'm not sure why) in Frankfurt, Germany, but I wasn't content to just visit the city. I arrived a few days early and took a low-cost ferry, cruising downstream on the Rhine River, and was awed by the castles I saw.

My love of travel continues and is undoubtedly a contributing factor to my business operations, building a hedge fund with a worldwide presence. Now that I am older, I revisit the same places, but I always walk around to experience them in new ways.

Perhaps Wichita State University was my first step to bridging the Eastern and Western business worlds.

• • •

I thrived at WSU and took advantage of seemingly all the courses the school offered. In my flat-fee program, after completing eighteen credit hours, every subsequent credit hour was free. I took a lot of classes in the social sciences: philosophy, anthropology, psychology, and more. I tried to learn how to play golf and the piano as well. I also took photography (before the advent of digital cameras) and enjoyed using the dark room to print my own pictures. Jennifer Chen was my model while I was experimenting with my photography skills.

Yes, I have to talk about Jennifer. She was my only Taiwanese friend in Wichita. We came to the English Center and were admitted to WSU at the same time. We even graduated on the same day. When I arrived on campus, I was wounded and lacked confidence. I was so lost and tried very hard to get oriented. I was just a boy, childish in many ways. Jennifer was the first woman in my life who pointed that out to me and taught me how

I should act to fit into this world. I also learned from her how to react to and treat a woman. She was the first person to show me the world of human relations.

We didn't see each other often but every time we got together, perhaps once a month or so, I tried to impress her with my new skills. For instance, I learned to cook. She tasted and tried all my experiments. I remember I made a special seafood dish that I had no way of reproducing. I called the dish "Thursday Morning." Why? Because I felt free and easy with that dish like a Thursday morning when I could sleep in without any morning classes. I tried to make Long Island Iced Tea using a Chinese medicine syrup. It tasted similar—but at the same time strange. Jennifer tried so many of the cocktails I created (and still turned out alright). She claimed I made the best blue margarita in town. I was so lucky to have her as my only Taiwanese friend and my best friend during my lonely days in Wichita. We remain best friends today.

I was also fortunate to have access to so many cultural events at WSU. I didn't have much money, but I always liked going to symphonies, plays, and operas. To gain admission, I volunteered to serve as an usher at those events. I was basically a young engineering nerd wearing a costume, standing in front of the theater gates, checking tickets, and saying, "Enjoy your show." But I got to sit down in the back and watch the performance for free after the doors were closed.

Generally, Wichita State required that you complete 128 credit hours to graduate. But to earn a degree in aerospace engineering required 138 credit hours because 10 hours of airplane design were added. I graduated with a total of 227 credit hours. (Yes, you read that right.) And I still earned cum laude honors with a 3.26 GPA. Unfortunately for today's students, they don't offer flat-fee programs anymore.

The more knowledge I gained, the more intellectually and emotionally fulfilled I became. I earned a bachelor's in aerospace engineering, and perhaps even more importantly, I regained my personhood and positive self-esteem at WSU. I am so grateful to the university and remain connected there.

During my senior year, my peers and I were focused on two missions: completing our final project required for graduation and securing jobs. The members of my engineering team opted to participate in a project jointly hosted by NASA (National Aeronautics and Space Administration) and the FAA (Federal Aviation Administration). Its aim was to create an alliance among government, industry, and academia in order to spur innovation in aviation. The project was named the Advanced General Aviation Transport Experiment, aka AGATE. Naturally, we named our team AGATE as well. In August 1997, the third annual AGATE national airplane design competition was held, and out of 192 participating schools worldwide, the Kansas team (composed of students from Wichita State, the University of Kansas, and Kansas State) took first place. It was my first big prize. I hung up my award certificate along with a check for $125 on the wall—even though I certainly could have used the money. I am never going to cash that check.

Our AGATE team was something special. Although we were taking part in one of the toughest projects of all, we had a great time and learned so much from the work and from one another. We were a truly international team, composed of Michael from Sweden, Chris and Jeff from the US, Francisco from Venezuela, Juan-Carlos from Spain, Chan from Malaysia, and, of course, Silver from Taiwan. I remember we used to stay up in the labs at NIAR (the National Institute of Aviation Research), located in the aerospace engineering corner of WSU, until five in the morning. Around 2:30 a.m., we would all be so tired, we would draw a lottery and see whose turn it was to buy everyone a bottle of Mountain Dew to give us juice for another three hours. It was a brotherhood bonding time. After we submitted the airplane design to the committee, we all went to the local bar and got drunk together and then slept for seventy-two hours straight.

Members of our AGATE Team were immediately hired by big aircraft companies, including Boeing and Raytheon, thereby completing mission number two for our senior year. Even *I* got a job offer from Boeing.

Not bad at all for Mr. 2.7, the Taiwanese high school failure!

After all these years, I always consider Wichita to be the place where I transformed from a naïve young boy into a more mature man. It was the turning point that got me ready to face the big world. I kept in contact with friends as well as WSU faculty after I left. In fact, in 2024, the tech support center at the newly completed WSU Barton Business School building was named after me, as I proudly contributed to its construction. And in September of that year, I was nominated and approved to be one of the advisors of the Barton School Dean's Fabulous 50 Board. Although I graduated from the engineering school, I thought I could help more with the business school in light of all the experience I have gathered over the years.

Upon graduating in 1997, I was still thirsty for more knowledge and wanted to broaden my career choices. An engineering career path seemed too short and shallow; you can only go so far in the profession. There is only one chief engineer in any given enterprise, and only a few other desirable options exist. I didn't want to limit myself to a dead-end career. However, an education in finance could lead to infinite career possibilities and advancement, and so that was my next pursuit.

I am very grateful that I had the chance to live in Wichita. It changed my life completely. I realized I was not stupid after all. Much more than that, I was outstanding in many ways, and I regained my confidence. Two things I discovered about myself during my time there: One, it turns out I have a photographic memory, especially as it pertains to numbers and also when memory is necessary to solve problems. For example, when we were calculating the lift force of an airplane, we usually had to refer to a big table of metrics specifying air density with respect to altitude. I didn't have to look up anything on the table; I remembered it all and still do. And two, I can see the essence of things by shifting through the chunk of garbage before it. I always know what the key point is even though there may be tons of noise masking it.

Both advantages, when combined, give me a boost to develop my business. I always know what to do and am always steps ahead of market trends, opportunities, or disasters. This also makes me a good poker player; I won several Texas Hold'em poker tournaments because of these qualities.

I guess I am not stupid after all.

I dreamed of being a business tycoon one day. It was a youthful fantasy that I didn't expect to ever become a reality. But now I can say, with humility, that I've achieved my ambitious goal.

When I applied to MBA programs, I asked one of my professors, Dr. Nagati, to write a letter of recommendation. I was unprepared for his response: "You are throwing away your engineering education! You are throwing away a guaranteed good income!" I was undeterred and applied to several universities and was tempted by an offer from Northeastern University in Boston.

However, I knew if I was going to study business and finance, the only place to learn was the financial capital not only of America but of the world: New York City. I packed up my car for yet another road trip; I was moving to New York to attend the renowned MBA program at Pace University's Lubin School of Business.

Goodbye for now, Kansas. I was on my way to the Big Apple!

4

New York: Moving to the Financial Capital of the World

When contemplating which graduate schools in the US I should pursue, I had decided to cast a wide net, applying to several business schools on the East and West Coasts. Even though I received many admissions offers, it was easy for me to make my choice; I realized that I absolutely had to be in New York City, the epicenter of the financial world, if I were serious about a business career.

The renowned MBA program at Pace's Lubin School seemed the smartest choice. It is in the heart of Manhattan's downtown financial district, which is always bustling with international activity. It was the perfect place to study for a business degree and launch a career. For similar reasons, Pace attracts a faculty that is composed of global leaders and heavy hitters.

I only studied for two weeks in the MBA program at Pace, but don't get the wrong impression—my short-lived participation in the program was not because I had chosen the wrong university or had quickly failed academically. It was because I learned a better option was available to me at Pace: I could earn a master's in investment management there, which I learned would be far more advantageous to me.

A classmate's suggestion prompted this change in the trajectory of my graduate studies. Corinna and I talked over a few days, and she convinced me I would be better off with a master of science instead of a master of business administration. She argued that to get an MBA, you study a wide range of business topics but nothing thoroughly. By contrast, when pursuing an MS, you concentrate intensively on one subject, gaining valuable expertise.

I think my classmate had ulterior, self-interested motives: She was studying for an MS and hoped I'd be her classmate and study partner. My English was better, I had the benefit of an engineering background, and I was more culturally acclimated to the US than she was. Corinna became a good friend. During our time in school, she tried to help me open up but failed. I enjoyed being alone too much. One day she knocked on my forehead: "Hello? Is anyone there?" She said I had probably moved to Earth from Mars. It was not that I didn't get the hint. I was in search of my true self and my ideal significant other. I needed time. She never wanted to talk to me again after I got married.

Even with her influence and cajoling, I decided to switch degree programs from an MBA to an MS in finance based on my own independent research and logical assessment of my career potential, background, and interests. At Tainan First High School, I was trained (albeit unhappily) to memorize and use my brain as a calculator. At Wichita State, I learned to think creatively and problem-solve effectively. Further, my self-assigned "curriculum" led me to read widely in the humanities and social sciences, deepening my knowledge in so many different disciplines.

These prior educational experiences, taken together, served me well at Pace, and the work was pleasurable and stimulating. Practical yet difficult business terminology and financial systems like modeling, derivatives, and determining valuations were easy for me to grasp, having mastered engineering language and concepts.

As I've said before, I had deliberately chosen to pursue dual degrees—first engineering, then business—to broaden my career options, better position me as a job candidate, and distinguish myself. The professors teaching in Pace's MS program were people I aspired to be like—leaders with real-world business experience, including CEOs and hedge fund managers—not ivory tower theoreticians.

As I touched on earlier, the faculty was an alphabet soup of global business leaders. My first macroeconomics professor was the former chair of Nasdaq. Another teacher worked for the Foreign Exchange Market (FX) of Citibank. It is an understatement to say that I learned a lot from these experienced men and women. Each had successfully applied what they were teaching to their careers. Thus, I gained practical and analytical knowledge to apply to my career as well.

TAKING A BITE OUT OF THE BIG APPLE

From Frank Sinatra to Billy Joel to Jay-Z, many musicians have crooned about the promise and possibilities that abound in New York City. It might be up to New York to offer opportunities that draw millions to its streets and skyscrapers, but how I would fare in the city was solely up to me. My money management skills, entrepreneurial spirit, and investment strategies all supported me during graduate school. Let me explain.

Although I chose a business degree program wisely, I was naïve about how expensive living in New York would be. My rent in Kansas for a one-bedroom apartment was $350 a month, so you can imagine the sticker shock I felt when a comparable apartment in Manhattan cost at least $2,500 per month. Even the boroughs of Brooklyn and Queens were prohibitively expensive.

Always practical and resourceful, I expanded my housing search to New Jersey and found a safe, clean neighborhood in Journal Square, Jersey City. The apartment building had a parking lot, so keeping my car wasn't a problem. It was also close to a Port Authority of New York and New Jersey (PATH) train stop that went directly to Manhattan, so I joined the throngs of commuters entering NYC from New Jersey each day. I settled into my routine of commuting, attending classes, and studying. I also took advantage of New York's cornucopia of cultural events—but more on that later.

Although the cost of living in Jersey City in the mid-1990s was much cheaper than in New York, it was still expensive. (Today, the area is more gentrified, and prices have skyrocketed.) I immediately set my mind on finding a job. One of my professors ran the tutoring center at Pace, so I interviewed for a position teaching math. He hired me on the spot for $5 an hour. After three days, he was so impressed with my work that he tripled my pay to $15 an hour. It's a paltry sum today, but thirty years ago, it represented a lot of money.

Business math was a piece of cake for me, and the professor heading the tutoring center probably thought I could elevate the quality and reputation of the program. Once, I was working with a student on his level-two calculus assignment and pointed out something incorrect. He was astonished that I immediately solved the problem by doing all the calculations in my head. Another time, a student came to me during finals saying he was a very quick learner. He showed me his math textbook and asked me to teach it to him from beginning to end. I threw him out.

The tutoring center was rarely busy, except for before midterms and final exams when stressed-out students lined up with questions. So I had a lot of time to myself. I read pleasure books and novels on quiet days. The only catch was that during exams, when the center was packed with students waiting to see me, I had my own studying to do.

My parents had no idea how expensive it was to live and study in the US, and the East Coast was in a whole different stratosphere. I asked them for tuition money, $8,000 per semester, and they agreed—but I didn't ask for living expenses; I was determined to make my own living and not depend on them. I've discussed my strained relationship with my parents and how they viewed me as an embarrassing failure. (I believe they both loved me, but I don't think they liked me.) I fully intended to make it here . . . and *anywhere*!

THE $8,000 INVESTMENT STRATEGY

To maximize my parents' $8,000 tuition contribution, I developed a system for making money. It started with not using the funds my parents sent me to pay tuition! Instead, I applied for several credit cards and charged the tuition against one of them. Then, each month, I would make a balance transfer to pay off one credit card with another, thus avoiding any interest charges.

Better yet, I made a lot of money! I opened an E*TRADE account and invested $8,000 in the stock market. Through a combination of luck and skill—especially my ability to calculate valuations and research and analyze financials—I generated positive returns. For example, I bought shares of a public hospital management company, which turned out to be the golden goose that tripled my investment. I had identified a US corporation managing hundreds of hospitals nationwide because I knew it could be exceedingly profitable. Unlike in Taiwan or China, where hospitals are philanthropic, not-for-profit enterprises, most US hospitals aim to generate revenue for their owners.

I posted my opinion on a Yahoo message forum that buying shares of that company was a good bet, and it generated a lot of discussion. I based my estimation on textbook-style valuation methods that contradicted the other comments on the message board. It turned out that I was correct and had made a good bet.

Out of the blue, a *Wall Street Journal* reporter called, asking if I had insider information. (Of course, I didn't!) I don't know how the journalist found my contact information, but he had the right phone number, and I had the right valuation number. I paid off my tuition and credit cards and had plenty left over to travel worldwide.

Even though I have the financial acumen to make educated investments, I am risk-averse and live debt-free. Today, I set modest growth targets of about 6 to 8 percent per annum for my personal portfolio, and this strategy has been quite successful over the years.

THE SCRAMBLED EGGS INCIDENT

Socially, I had integrated well while living in Wichita, although, as I mentioned, 70 percent of its population is white. So I was unprepared for the scrambled eggs incident in my Jersey City neighborhood as I came home from school one day. Two Black kids, no more than ten years old, threw raw eggs at me for no apparent reason other than I was a foreigner with a different skin color. Stunned, I didn't know how to react; I just turned around, went back to my apartment, and washed up.

Of course, my feelings were hurt, but I figured they were just kids who didn't know what they were doing. This kind of incident occurred a few times, but I took them in stride because, though memorable, they weren't the norm.

THE TRIP TO THE MORGUE

On the positive side of the ledger, I had more friends in New York than in Wichita, including students from NYU and Columbia. Some became close female friends, but I never had a girlfriend in college or grad school.

Sometimes, I felt that I "should" have a relationship, as it seemed to be a way of life for young people in the city to do things in pairs. Some women were romantically interested in me, but I didn't want to compromise my goal to be in a meaningful relationship with someone who genuinely understood me. I'm comfortable in my own skin, and being alone didn't mean I was lonely.

I did have one close Taiwanese friend in New York, Travis Chen. We shared many interests and loved movies, prompting meaningful and spirited discussions. Early one morning, I was awakened by a surprise call from an unfamiliar voice: Travis's uncle. He got right to the point, asking if I was Silver and if I knew that Travis had died the night before.

Apparently, Travis was diagnosed with a heart condition of some sort when he was younger, and that night, he drank some red wine, smoked a cigar, and then—*boom*—at three in the morning, he dropped dead from a heart attack. I was shocked and saddened.

Travis must have listed me as an emergency contact and his uncle made a bold request: Would I go to the morgue to identify Travis's body? The uncle lived in California and couldn't get to New York immediately. Of course, I was willing to oblige under the circumstances—Travis was a really good guy. I identified the body and helped organize the memorial, coordinating everything with his parents and relatives. It was a sad ending to a short life and a short-lived friendship.

TALKING TO STRANGERS

Before moving to New York, I was a shy, hesitant young engineering nerd who had recently regained some confidence and self-esteem. I didn't have any experience with encountering strangers, regardless of their race or nationality. In Wichita, I had been alone reading my books and watching my movies most of the time. When I came to New York, it was overwhelming! I still remember the time when someone heard I'd just moved to the Big Apple from Kansas, and said to me, "I heard you guys still ride horses to work. Is that true?" I tried to open my heart and embrace the new world, but I never knew how to fit in. Until, that is, I met two young women who changed my life. Nothing romantic, mind you. Rather, Irene and Annie became my best friends during that period in New York, and we still remain very good friends today after twenty-eight years.

I met Irene on a flight back to Taiwan from New York. I had used up all my saved credit card miles in exchange for a reward seat in business class. I was so excited. I opened the screen in front of me and started watching all the movies I could. They included *The Man in the Iron Mask* (1998), with Leonardo DiCaprio, Gabriel Byrne, John Malkovich, and Gérard Depardieu. It was very popular at the time, and the cast was excellent. But all the while I was sitting there, I couldn't help noticing the beautiful girl sitting next to me. I must have rehearsed how to talk to someone like her—a stranger on an airplane—a thousand times. I gawkishly turned and said, "Have you watched this movie yet? It is about the Three Musketeers." She smiled and said she hadn't, but that sparked a conversation. I would soon discover that Irene was a rising junior at Columbia University and probably the most talented person I had ever met. She is a great singer and even auditioned for Kim in *Miss Saigon* and Éponine in *Les Misérables*. She is now a very famous painter in Asia. She miraculously cured my shyness around strangers.

I was introduced to Annie by my Pace friend Veny on a short trip to West Point one Saturday. Annie was a student from NYU, and she made quite an impression on me even though we didn't talk much that first day. I asked for her phone number and all I got was a fax number. (Younger readers might need to look up what those were.) I wrote her a page of self-introduction and, again, I must have rehearsed a thousand times what I would say. I was so shy and hesitant to initiate a conversation with any stranger. But I did it. I stepped out of my comfort zone and we became best friends.

One night I was packing for a trip to Frankfurt the next morning when I received a call from Annie saying she'd lost the key to her apartment, and she couldn't get a hold of her landlord. She asked if I could pick her up. It was two in the morning. She was being considered for a role in a theater production of *My Fair Lady*, so we stayed up the rest of the night rehearsing for her audition and waiting for her landlord to call back.

I am very grateful for these two fine ladies who inspired me to spend more time with others instead of being by myself most of the time. I've developed the ability to talk with any stranger since meeting them.

SEEING *LES MISÉRABLES* ON BROADWAY TWENTY-ONE TIMES!

New York City served up a cultural feast of opera, concerts, theater, indie films, and art. Even though I was studying and working hard, I still had a lot of leisure time and made the most of it. I went to Lincoln Center often to attend the opera and listen to classical music. I also visited movie theaters nearby that showed foreign and independent art films unavailable at mainstream theaters.

I didn't mind going to these performances alone; in fact, I did so happily. I vividly remember being at an Italian restaurant near Lincoln Center and telling the hostess I wanted a table for one before the show started. I still have a picture of that place and time in my mind's eye.

I didn't have much money, but I figured out how to go to events on a budget. I spent hours in line at the TKTS booth in Times Square, which sold steeply discounted same-day and next-day tickets. It was easy to get good, cheap, single seats.

I adored the play *Les Mis*! After watching it twenty-one times, I had memorized every line and could sing every song! The show appealed to my twin loves: the arts and history. I read many books about the French Revolution and was fascinated by underworld economics, the hidden, dark markets where commoners buy and sell illegal goods.

FROM LIVING ON MANHATTAN ISLAND TO HOPPING ISLANDS IN GREECE

I will always consider New York my home. I have two other bases—one in Kaohsiung, Taiwan, and one in Hong Kong—but whenever I return to Manhattan, I feel like I am coming home. After graduating from Pace in 1999, however, it made sense for me to go back to Taiwan for a while.

The university had a job-placement office, but it was too complicated to get offers as an international student without green-card status. I did have some interviews that served as good practice for later interactions. Additionally, there wasn't a high demand for business school graduates in the US at that time; if I had wanted to work in engineering, it would have been a different story.

But before I left New York for Taiwan, I went to Greece for about a month. I used the money I'd made in the stock market to fund my travels. I visited the Greek islands, strolled through museums, and saw all the ruins.

Again, this experience combined my passions for adventure, seeing the world, and a love of history, literature, and art. Greece particularly appealed to me because I was able to experience sights *and* sites—to see the country's stunning land and seascape and also experience the many places I had read about in history and mythology books. It is a place of rare beauty. Even today, out of the fifty countries I have visited, Greece is still ranked number one on my list.

THE INTERNATIONAL WALL OF POSTCARDS

Back in New York, it was time to start packing for Taiwan. It didn't take much to divest myself of my possessions. I took my car to a local repair shop and asked what they'd pay for it. They offered me $7,500, and I said, "Sold!" I probably could have gotten closer to $8,500, but the ease and expeditiousness of the transaction was worth the discount.

My small studio apartment in Jersey City didn't contain much to dispose of, and I readily gave away my desk and stereo to classmates. However, I deeply regret not taking my guitar with me—I put it in the apartment's recycling area, hoping someone would take good care of it for me. I packed my books to bring with me and, all in all, I had about thirty boxes to send via cargo ship to Taiwan.

I kept my most highly prized possession: postcards from around the world, which had covered a big wall in the apartment. Whenever and wherever I traveled—Milan, London, Paris, Greece—I bought a picture postcard and sent it to myself. Then, I would stick them on my wall with removable tacky clay. In the center of the wall was a large poster of Irène Jacob, the beautiful, talented, French-Swiss actress who worked with Polish film director Krzysztof Kieślowski and French director Louis Malle. She may be best known for her role in *Red* (1994), one of the Three Colors trilogy. (My younger daughter, Irene, is her namesake.)

I began the postcard collection because I wanted a souvenir from wherever I had traveled. Postcards had the advantages of being cheap and portable. I made them even more meaningful because I would write a note to myself and affix the country's postal stamp. It felt cool to do that, and the postcards captured precious memories.

ENTERING THE JOB MARKET IN TAIPEI, TAIWAN

As I mentioned in chapter 1, when I returned to Taiwan in 1999, technology was booming there, and the stock market was rising every day. Despite a 7.6-magnitude earthquake on September 21, 1999, the high-tech sector, including the semiconductor industry, survived and strengthened. Taiwan made 80 to 90 percent of all advanced computer chips globally. It was an excellent place to seek my first full-time job.

I interviewed at several investment banks and securities firms and quickly learned that my dual educational credentials—an engineering and a finance degree—gave me a decided advantage in the job market. Many people who study finance in Taiwan do so to start a business, and many who seek jobs in finance have only studied liberal arts. But with my dual degrees, I was uniquely positioned as a candidate. Instead of competing with twenty other people for a single job, I was sought-after.

At one investment bank in Taipei, I interviewed in three departments: initial public offerings (IPOs), secondary public offerings (SPOs), and institutional sales. The leaders of all three departments met with me together and *asked* which department I'd like to work in. It was a great privilege to have a choice! I chose to work on SPOs for companies that were already publicly traded, raising additional money through secondary stock offerings.

My readjustment to Taiwan and what I learned to do (and not do) while working at the investment bank was quite interesting, but more on that later.

Suffice it to say that I would apply the lessons from both my formal education in the US and my informal education at the investment management company to each future business endeavor I undertook. I also applied my ethical principles, born of my core values of right and wrong and my distrust of governments and banks, to run honorable, debt-free organizations.

5

Taiwan: Investment Banking, Naïveté, and Choices

As I was writing the first draft of this chapter, Taiwan was in the middle of a terrible November typhoon, Kong-rey, which produced record-breaking rainfall, flooding, and wind speeds comparable to those of a Category 4 hurricane landfall. Since Taiwan is mountainous, the storm created massive mudslides that covered entire beaches. By the time it ended, Typhoon Kong-rey had injured over five hundred people and resulted in at least two deaths.[1]

Typhoons and earthquakes have always been a way of life in Southeast Asia; however, the weather patterns have changed and worsened in the forty or so years since I was a child. We used to have four distinct seasons, but now it seems as if we only have the lead-up to either a scorching-hot summer or a hot summer with only slight temperature variations. Previously, typhoon season was between June and early September, but now, it extends to November and beyond.

I suppose you could say that as I've changed personally and grown professionally for the better, Taiwan's climate has changed for the worse!

THE NEW KID IN THE ROOM

After moving back to Taiwan from New York in August 1999, I would have ideally liked to accept the offer extended to me by the US securities firm Merrill Lynch, which had Asian branches, but they only had private banking opportunities open, and I was determined to learn more about the corporate finance side of investment banking. Thankfully, other offers ensued, as, again, my dual engineering and finance degrees were viewed as an asset. In September of that same year, I accepted a job at a securities company. They were one of the largest investment banks in Taiwan at the time, and, as I mentioned in the previous chapter, I was honored to have the choice of working either in IPOs, SPOs, or institutional sales. At age twenty-seven—with very limited investment banking experience—I was asked to interview each department head instead of them interviewing me!

Most people want to work on IPOs because converting a private company to a public one seems exciting and meaningful. However, the success rate of IPOs is poor; only 10 to 30 percent of deals go through. I joined the SPO department instead, working with public companies seeking to raise additional money by issuing bonds, convertible bonds, or other securities. These were mature companies, so I got the experience I sought in corporate finance as an analyst determining valuations for new offerings.

Not only were the companies mature, but their leaders were also seasoned and, most certainly, older than me. As the inexperienced "newbie," I often felt intimidated by the stature of the CEOs, CFOs, and chairpersons I encountered. Many ran big, well-known companies led by famous people, and they received favorable media attention—newspaper headline stories, TV appearances, and so forth.

As I became more experienced, my respect for these titans of business eroded because I learned how many of them became so rich, and I was shocked. Let me explain.

BEHIND CLOSED DOORS

I attended many closed meetings with CEOs, CFOs, and chairs, even though I was just a junior analyst. My role was to quietly sit to the side and take notes. (Whenever I interacted with company leaders, a senior member of the organization would accompany me.) When the leaders in these private meetings discussed the company's strategy for its SPO, determining how they would price the new shares to be issued to the public, *they almost always seemed to already have a target price* in mind! Talk about gaming the system!

I listened attentively but wasn't directly involved in the discussions about strategies to raise money and set stock prices. My job was to write a report, providing a well-reasoned analysis of company valuations and pricing models. My reports were fact-based, and the mathematical calculations were accurate and well-documented.

When asked for my analysis, I spoke up, clearly and logically explaining my pricing recommendations. I knew my valuations were correct and fair, but my suggestions were *never* heeded—it didn't matter what I proposed.

I was naïve. I had no idea how things were regularly done in the investment banking world, so it surprised me when private companies did things that did not seem entirely legal or ethical—including manipulating stock prices for personal gain. For example, if the stock was trading at $50 per share, they would use various methods to jack up its price to $80 per share. Thus, the company's valuation increased, and the company would raise more money and issue fewer shares, making the bankers a lot more money.

One common and perfectly legal way for a company to raise money is to issue convertible bonds (CBs). A CB allows the holder to convert the debt obligation to equity at a predetermined price, generally set at a discount to market. The bonds are sold to banks, and the company must repay the bank with interest before the bond becomes due.

But now comes the tricky part: The bank sells *the right to convert the debt to equity* to the company's major shareholders. The company then makes some public announcements, driving up the price of the stock. When the stock is higher than the options' strike price, the major shareholders distribute the stock options to the employees, who then have the right to exercise the options at a substantial profit.

In Taiwan, the listed company's C-suite executives and employees typically want to be paid with stock options, not a fixed salary. The major shareholders can distribute the stock options to the employees in any way they want. Since the stock options are not distributed by the company, when the options are issued, they will be taxed at a more favorable capital gains rate and not as ordinary income.

Since the stock options are not being issued or distributed by the company, the major shareholders will have the option (no pun intended) to pick and choose who will be given the options and how many to distribute. Of course, the major shareholders will often keep the lion's share for themselves. While this is a win-win for the company and its employees, this strategy seems to rip-off other investors.

I was so green and naïve back then! As I said, I had zero idea that these games were played at investment banks. I could not complain or speak up . . . or I would have been in big trouble. Seriously!

MORE GAMES PLAYED FOR GAINS

There are also numerous other stock-manipulation schemes—none of which I've ever engaged in. But over the years, I've witnessed them in action. For example, there are "pump-and-dump" schemes. This happens when investment bankers buy stock at artificially low prices and then launch an extensive marketing campaign promoting the virtues of the stock—similar to the price-pumping example I mentioned previously—which likely results in a significant price increase. Then, the bankers sell the stock. When the hype doesn't materialize, the stock price falls. The investors who bought the stock based on the hype have lost their investment, while those behind the manipulation profit.

"Front-running" is another scheme whereby bankers are privy in advance to a significant favorable or unfavorable announcement, such as a report on the company's unexpected profitability or loss. They then buy or sell the stock accordingly and make a profit.

Because the Taiwanese government regulated securities firms, my family and I were subject to the same regulations. At the time, the regulations were loose, and there were no strict laws prohibiting profiting from insider information. Despite how lax enforcement was, I was considered an insider; I could not buy or sell shares without declaring the transaction. But people did this all the time, and no one went to jail for it back then.

All this manipulation and shadiness was entirely against my ethics. I knew how to determine a stock's fair market value but saw how share prices were unfairly and dishonestly manipulated. My on-the-job education was eye-opening. What I learned in those closed-door meetings significantly impacted my thinking and later business dealings—I understood how things were too often being done and, more importantly, I understood what *not* to do.

I learned not to trust the stock market, and since that experience, I've never purchased a single share of stock in Taiwan! Only recently, at age fifty-two, have I bought stock—but only in the US.

DECISIONS, DECISIONS, DECISIONS

In 2000, about six months into my tenure, the company I was working for was acquired by another securities firm.

My first job in investment banking gave me a clear sense of the internal turmoil M&As can unleash.

The company became chaotic, leaving me and my colleagues anxious, confused, and demoralized. As you'll recall, only a few months earlier I was offered with three positive options: to work on IPOs, SPOs, or sales. Suddenly, I faced three negative choices for my *next* career move: stay, leave with my boss, or go home to Kaohsiung.

The new entity offered me a job, and, at the same time, my boss decided to leave and move to another large investment bank. He recruited me and some of my colleagues to go with him, promising salary increases. The third option was to leave Taipei and return home to work with my father in his electric scooter business.

I debated my choices for almost two months—with myself, my colleagues, and my family. Choosing my next step was agonizing; sadly, none of the choices were good. Each carried problematic risks and low rewards. But one seemed like the least unpleasant of the three. Ultimately, my filial Chinese sense of duty and the slight possibility of pulling off a successful IPO for my father's company conspired to bring me home.

A CHOP STAMP SEALED MY FUTURE

I didn't anticipate the magnitude of the events that would ensue when I returned home from Taipei. No one did.

I had not lived in Kaohsiung for many years. While studying in the US, I only visited during my two-month summer vacations. My parents treated me better than they did when I was growing up because I was doing well in America. Still, we were like strangers.

On a visit home from Pace, I first learned about the $10 million business loan I had guaranteed, which I described in chapter 1. We were eating dinner and having a superficial conversation, and either my mother or sister casually mentioned the guarantee: "How was your day and, by the way, you might owe $10 million." I didn't give the situation any further thought and returned to New York feeling unencumbered.

I don't think my parents ever intended to tell me about the guarantee, and they certainly hadn't asked my permission to sign the loan documents with that stipulation intact. That's simply not how Chinese parents behave. Children are expected to obey, and the eldest son has special obligations; in this case, I was required to be my father's business loan guarantor. No questions asked. As I've said before, the banks think that if a son is on the hook to repay a loan, the parents will do everything in their power to prevent defaulting. It's a hostage situation. Simple as that.

For all intents and purposes, my parents went behind my back. They took it upon themselves to make a chop stamp with *my* name! In China or in Taiwan, a personal chop stamp is used in lieu of a handwritten signature to authorize documents. These chops are traditionally made of stone or wood and have the person's name calligraphed in Chinese characters. When the chop is dipped in red ink and affixed to a document, the deal is sealed. I have kept that one particular chop stamp with me all these years to remind myself of what happened back then and what life lessons it taught me.

If only a new Taiwanese government hadn't been installed in May 2000 and reversed the previous regime's policies supporting climate-friendly initiatives and businesses, my father's company would have succeeded. There would be no need to call the loan, and I never would have known or cared about the fact that I had assumed liability in absentia. But that wasn't how events unfolded.

As you now know, when my father's electric scooter company started to fail, I was desperate to find another job to support my family. I held some teaching positions here and there, but the government garnished my salary, leaving me with next to nothing to live on.

My father explicitly told me I couldn't leave his company. He said, "We are a family. If the ship is going down, we all go down together." If I had criticized or disobeyed him, I would have been considered unethical and an outcast in society. I was silenced at the company I had just left and now I was being silenced by my family, too.

Although it is no consolation, my colleagues at my former job didn't fare well either. In 2000, tech companies started to crash. The dot-com bubble burst, and the stock market collapsed in the US and Taiwan. It was a terrible time for investment banking, and many of my peers were laid off and forced to seek new jobs.

It was a double-punch typhoon: The worldwide economy and Taiwanese policies were spinning uncontrollably, rocking many people's lives and livelihoods—my own included.

6

Tyranny Back Home: Working with My Father

To be blunt, the time I spent in Kaohsiung from 2000 to 2002 brings back painful and dark memories.

In the beginning, it wasn't all that bad because the product my father's company produced—electric scooters—was within the purview of my technical engineering expertise. Further, the business was still going well then. As you will recall, the government was incentivizing environmentally friendly products. My father initially placed me in the research and development (R&D) department, where I enjoyed working with all the other engineers on the technical side of the business.

Designing and developing electric vehicles relies on two kinds of engineering skills: mechanical and electrical. The mechanical aspect involves the wheels and other moving parts, and electrical engineering deals with batteries, controls, and other technological components. I was proficient at both and good at synthesizing the two disciplines.

I appreciated that my father wanted me to gain experience and learn how his products were designed—it was an opportunity to apply and hone the skills I had acquired as an undergraduate. But he soon pulled me from the engineering position to become the chairman's special assistant, working directly under him. In Taiwan, the special assistant's job was to shadow and observe the chairman; this was my father's way of showing me his company's operations. Implicit in his decision was the expectation that someday I would take over the company. Practically speaking, though, my role was more like that of a consultant—someone who was allowed to observe but only give limited input.

When the time came to prepare for the launch of the company's initial public offering, I finally assumed a leadership role; I had the relevant experience and mental agility to do so. But as I've said before, the ruling government party changed and brought along a tsunami of previous-policy reversals. There were no longer any sources of support for products or businesses seeking to mitigate the effects of climate change—not from the government, the banks, or the securities firms. Incentives for electric vehicle production and consumer purchasing no longer existed. Consequently, our IPO effort was a massive failure.

STEERING A SINKING SHIP

As a result of those shocking developments, I assumed my third role in the business, progressing (or, you could say, regressing) from engineer to business assistant to a one-man cleanup crew. I was now focused on fund-raising efforts to keep the business afloat. This was also a matter of self-preservation; there was truth to my father's earlier statement that if he went down, the whole family would go down. I was also motivated by two personal attributes: my desire to learn and to succeed at everything I undertook.

There was only one way to keep the company alive: a significant cash infusion. I prepared a detailed business plan that reported and analyzed two aspects of the company: its business operations and engineering specifications. The plan set forth well-documented projections based on my financial analysis. It also included technical details about what kind of product we could make now, and in the future, and their advantages.

Armed with my business plan, I looked for traditional and novel funding sources. I approached venture capitalists, private lenders, large investment banks, individuals, and other investors. I began negotiations with those who demonstrated interest, and both sides—me and the potential investors—engaged in due diligence. This went on for roughly six months; however, all the prospects lost interest as it became evident that even with their support, our business model was still largely dependent on government backing and cash we didn't have.

The most frustrating part for me was that I *already knew* continuing with our current business model wouldn't work without such backing. The reality was that we had to alter our operations significantly. We couldn't survive without changing!

However, my father was averse to change. I wrote him a twenty-page personal letter—an internal memo explaining my reasoning and outlining an improved business model. But my father was so stubborn and set in his ways, he wouldn't even listen to my ideas. We kept pushing back and forth like this for an entire year.

I finally told him directly, "If we don't change, the company will die!" Still, it was like talking to a brick wall. His brusque, condescending response was, "What do *you* know? You're just a kid! You've only been in the company for a year!" He'd always thought I was stupid—ever since my early school days. (Remember: I was "Mr. 2.7.")

The company went down so fast that it was head-spinning. Even so, I wasn't surprised. I had tried to forestall what was an inevitable failure. But the situation was hopeless . . . and I was, in the end, helpless.

Without cash, the company couldn't pay rent or salaries. All our debtors came after us, as did the bank. And some mafiosos actually came after us, too. The vultures were feasting on our carcass. I tried to help my father negotiate new terms to buy some time, but, unsurprisingly, he rejected all my suggestions. We were besieged by lawsuits. My sister took on some of the work and asked for my advice, but she didn't heed it either. I honestly don't know if my ideas would have worked had my father or sister implemented them. But my recommendations would have at least given the business a fighting chance.

So now, as the eldest son and guarantor of my father's bank loans, I owed $10 million!

SUFFOCATING CHINESE FAMILY EXPECTATIONS

I had given up my finance career and lucrative earning potential to help my family clean up their business mess—for two full years! I was so stressed that I couldn't breathe. And perhaps worst of all, I had no physical space to myself.

During this entire time, I lived with my family in their house. Not because I wanted to, but because Taiwanese culture (and my lack of income) demanded it. However, eventually, to save my sanity, I did something considered highly disrespectful and morally unethical: I rented a tiny apartment. It was only ten kilometers away, but my father was furious. (He was also bewildered—how could I leave when I had a room under his roof?) He didn't understand how tense, exhausted, and suffocated I felt.

My father expressed his fury not by yelling or swearing at me; instead, he responded in typical, traditional Taiwanese fashion. He gave me "the look," silently staring into my eyes for at least ten minutes—maybe more. That look is more painful than a physical slap in the face.

Finally, he said, "It is unfortunate that you say this . . ." I think if he had finished the sentence and expressed his full sentiments, he would have said, "It is unfortunate for me to have a son like you." Of course, my mother sided with him.

I left and moved out my parents' house the next day.

My father believed I had violated the sanctity of our family. We didn't talk for nearly a year, and he considered it my fault that our connection was cut. He never even visited my new place.

I'm fortunate that I had the fortitude not to hurt myself or do anything crazy. Although I was terribly frustrated, I was also incredibly strong. You would think that after almost losing one son to an overdose, my parents would cherish me. But that's not the Chinese mentality.

As I relayed earlier, soon after my father's IPO failed in 2000, he was diagnosed with stage 4 lung cancer and died shortly thereafter. My relatives had berated me for working in Taipei instead of staying behind and caring for my sick father. However, I wasn't being an ungrateful son; I was just trying to survive.

As I said, I was suffocating. I believed if I could get off the sinking ship in Kaohsiung alive, I could save my other family members. It was the same principle as putting on your own oxygen mask before helping others in an aircraft emergency.

MENTAL ESCAPISM: BEYOND A ROOM OF MY OWN

The combination of my father's death, my estrangement from my family, and my poor financial condition elevated my stress level through the stratosphere. The best way to accurately describe my state of mind is that I was "stuck in limbo."

As usual, I turned to movies and books to occupy my mind, and distract, enlighten, and entertain me. (I would have liked to travel, but I had no money.) I rented so many movies in 2002 and 2003 that I can't remember a particular favorite. But I do remember that the 1994 book *The Warren Buffett Way*, by Robert G. Hagstrom, made a strong impression on me. It describes the central tenets of Buffett's "business-driven investment" strategy.

A few simple principles that Buffett espoused still stick in my mind:

- look for value,
- do it early,
- don't sell,
- don't invest into anything you don't understand.[2]

As I was plotting my future during this dark time, Buffett inspired me not only to climb out of the abyss but also to shine. This wasn't my financial investment strategy—I didn't have a penny then. It was a psychological entreaty to wisely invest my time, efforts, and emotions; I decided that I should pursue value and be patient, and time would do its magic. Buffett's strategy is my financial investment approach now that I have millions of pennies!

I also read Jim Rogers's 2003 book *The Adventure Capitalist.* As a lifelong traveler, Rogers believed that to understand a country's economic conditions, you must go see it in person. You gain more insight that way than from reading *The Wall Street Journal.*[3] This attitude may seem to contradict my passion for books. On the contrary, reading and traveling complement each other. There's an old Chinese saying, 讀萬券書行萬里路, which means that traveling ten thousand miles is as important as reading ten thousand books.

GAINING HEDGE FUND EXPERIENCE

While still working for my father, in those days when it was evident that his business couldn't be resuscitated, I started to teach finance part-time at various universities. These positions paid poorly, and when you subtracted the one-third taken by the Taiwanese government to pay off my debt, I netted next to nothing. It was difficult for me to even get these ill-paying teaching positions because my debt tarnished my reputation as a finance professor. However, from 2003 to 2013, I taught intermittently in the finance graduate school at National Kaohsiung University of Science and Technology, one of Taiwan's best and oldest universities.

I persisted in looking for jobs and was offered a position as a quantitative financial engineer at the hedge fund ThetaSoft Limited. The year 2002 marked the first time Taiwan had allowed trading index options. I managed a team of eight people, developing arbitrage trading models—the buying and selling of assets in different financial markets. I had learned the basic theory behind arbitrage while studying at Pace, but Theta was my first actual experience building the models. I alone created about 190 different models; most (if not all) are still in use today.

However, I only worked at Theta for about a year. Why would I leave a job I was well-prepared for and where I was doing interesting work with a talented team? The answer is simple: The traders often deviated from my models in the emotional heat of the boiler room where trading took place, and the emotions bred unsavory manipulations. I was unjustly blamed for financial losses. So, as President Harry Truman famously said, "If you can't stand the heat, get out of the kitchen."[4]

Nevertheless, during that period I gained firsthand experience with stock index and stock options trading models. I spent countless nights developing computer models, doing experiments, and running simulations. I tried buying a basket of stocks and hedging it by writing an index call option or buying a put option. I tried different variations of what we called a *straddle strategy* by selling call options and put options at the same time and hedging that by buying or selling index future contracts.

When I started doing this in 2002 and 2003, computational trading models were still very new to the world, especially for arbitrage and hedging trading opportunities. Allow me to generally explain how this works.

Let's say I bought a kilogram of 99.99 percent pure gold in Tokyo and at the very same time I sold a kilogram of 99.99 percent pure gold in New York. It would seem as if the overall holdings netted out and I no longer had any gold in my pocket. But because the price of gold in Tokyo was determined by supply and demand locally, as was the price in New York, and because the USD/JPY conversion rate changes every second, there is always a small price difference. I figured, if I could use a computer trading system to capture the small difference and buy and sell such gold simultaneously, I'd make a profit without any risk. This is what we call arbitrage trading. If I am buying 1 kilogram of gold in Tokyo but only sell 0.8 kg in New York, then it is hedged trading. It all depends on the portion and what the numbers indicate we should do. We can use the same theory on almost everything. There will be more inconsistency in prices when trading cross countries, cross currency, and cross market; therefore there will be more opportunity and profit as long as I can find the right correlation between the commodities.

Trading on currencies is another example of this. As of this writing, the USDX (USD index) is weighted at 57.6 percent for EUR, 13.6 percent for JPY, 11.9 percent for GBP, 9.1 percent for CAD, 4.2 percent for SEK, and 3.6 percent for CHF. That means, theoretically, one USD should be equal to the USD value of the respective currencies combined. However, this is not a perfect world and local currencies are determined in their own economic conditions. This allows a great deal more room for arbitrage or hedge trading. I could buy currencies according to the percentage and then short sell USDX futures if I saw a profit opportunity.

One approach emerged as the best and most profitable back when I started experimenting with different models: playing around with Taiwan weighted stock index futures and options against the Taiwan index futures traded in Singapore SIMEX.

However, the cross-border, cross-market transactions created inefficiencies in contract valuations. That set up the perfect condition to make arbitrage profits. Despite the fact that I couldn't take the heat of the kitchen (the boiler room), I still consider 2002 a turning point for me as I transitioned from hopeless limbo to getting back on my feet in the high financial industry.

I regained my confidence. And for that, I am eternally grateful.

TEACHING IS LEARNING

I'm not sure when I realized that teaching was both a calling and a lifeline for me. Perhaps it was when I was working for ThetaSoft, doing financial engineering trade modeling, and several university finance professors invited me to teach at their respective universities. Passing on my real-life experience in the financial industry felt good.

But I was super nervous before I ever taught my first class. I was a very shy nerd in many ways. Although my two fine lady friends in New York, Irene and Annie, had cured my fear of talking to strangers years earlier, I still couldn't speak in front of a group. When I was preparing for those first teaching positions, I wrote detailed scripts, including every word I should say. I still have those notes from my earliest days as a part-time professor. I even jotted down when to pause and when to tell a joke, and I wrote the jokes down word for word. One time, I was talking too fast and reached the end of my script only halfway through the class. A very long silence followed—I had no idea what else I should say. I quickly searched through my memory bank of experiences and started to talk without a script. From then on, I no longer had to write down everything in order to speak comfortably in public. I was cured of that fear, too.

Since then, I have learned another valuable skill: I am able to explain very complex concepts to anyone by using very simple words they can understand. This new skill has been super important in my career. As I mentioned in chapter 3, I know I can see through a mess and capture its essence. I also have a photographic memory and am very good with numbers. And now, I can speak to strangers in public using language that people easily comprehend. I have applied my teaching skills outside of the classroom and they've helped shape my various business ventures, most notably the founding of Hyperion Capital Management and Siegfried Capital Group. Moreover, these skills helped establish who I am and all I have accomplished in my private life, too.

A BREATH OF FRESH AIR AND SUNLIGHT

I want to loop back here to describe some pivotal *positive* events, as my personal life wasn't all darkness and depression.

In 2000, a month after I moved back to Kaohsiung to work for my father, I met the woman who would become my wife—Wen-Ya Li. She has gone by the name Doriya Li her whole life. In Taiwan, we tend to find ourselves an American name, so it is easier for others to pronounce and remember. She thought of using Doris but wanted to add her first name *ya*. So, she combined Doris and Ya and became Doriya.

A female friend was instrumental in making the match, casually saying, "Hey, Silver, I think there's a person you might be interested in knowing." She gave each of us the other's email address. Doriya sent group emails with interesting articles, and I received them because she had added me to her contact list. After that, Doriya and I started to exchange emails directly.

Doriya worked in Taipei, and, like me, was from Kaohsiung. I asked if she would like to meet for lunch one day when I was in Taipei. She agreed to meet "as friends," giving me the impression that she had plenty of suitors and wasn't looking for a serious relationship, which was fine.

I remember the exact date I met Doriya: April 29, 2000. I learned three things about her immediately: She was very pretty, she was very spontaneous, and she was very smart.

At lunch, Doriya told me she worked for a well-regarded investment magazine and asked if I knew anything about investing. Without waiting for an answer, she spoke passionately about finance, stocks, bonds, and so much more. I was amused because she didn't know I had a graduate finance degree and built trading models. However, our shared interests were a promising sign.

Not only do I remember the exact date, but I also remember what I ate! I ordered a seafood pasta dish with white sauce. Habitually, I saved my favorite part—the squid—for last and ate the pasta first. As I began eating, I noticed Doriya staring at the squid, and in the next instant, she was eating it! "You don't want that?" she said with the squid already in her mouth. I was shocked. You don't do that to a person you are just meeting for the first time. I immediately changed my flight back to Kaohsiung from 2:30 p.m. to 6:00 p.m. I needed to know more about this strange girl.

After the lunch incident, we walked around and came across the Hess Bookstore. We wandered in, randomly talking about books. I pointed to a long shelf and told her I had read every book on it. She surely thought I was just embellishing to impress a girl. A while later, she realized I had told her the truth: I had read every single book on that full shelf *more than once*. She learned I never exaggerate.

Then we had coffee in a nearby movie theater before I headed to the airport to return to Kaohsiung. We saw a poster of *The Matrix* (1999), and Doriya started talking about the film and how she liked Keanu Reeves and the sci-fi effects. I shared my thoughts and feelings about the movie, too. I explained the meaning of Zen and the deeper interpretations of different dimensions and ways of thinking about where we are and what we are. She was stunned and speechless. That is when I knew I had her! She said she had discussed this movie with many people, and I was the only one who didn't talk about kung fu fighting and special effects.

Sometimes I compare *The Matrix* with *The Truman Show* (1998), except the latter didn't elaborate on what happened after Truman left the matrix (the set). When I was teaching at a university MBA program, I always offered everything I knew. I taught the students the truth, and it often backfired. I should have given them options to take the red or the blue pill, as was Neo's choice in *The Matrix*. Instead, I told them the world they saw was not the real world that existed. Maybe sometimes, or most of the time, people just don't want to know the truth.

I had a student who was a branch manager for a major bank in Taiwan. I explained everything I knew about how the banking system worked. At first, she was excited. She said I had opened her eyes, and that she learned so much from me. A few months later, she came to me and said point-blank she wished she had never met me. After taking my class, she couldn't manage the bank the way she had before. The branch revenue went down quickly, and she was barely holding on to her job. Most of the branches of the banks are carrying duty to sell wealth management products to their customers, such as mutual funds or insurance policies. After taking my classes, she realized it was wrong to do that by following the banks' order. Her husband and others blamed her for that. And she blamed me for showing her the world. Many people should simply take the blue pill and live the lives they are happy with.

After that, I started to hold back, never teaching students everything I know.

But all that aside, there was no doubt that Doriya and I would have a second date. As we figured out when to meet, I told her my birthday was the following week. "Then let's meet up for your birthday on the seventh of May," she said. Doriya suggested we have dinner in Taipei and then go to Jioufen, a beautiful mountainous town in the far north overlooking the ocean. She had stayed once at a friend's house there, and she remembered it in great detail—the large windows, spectacular harbor views, room layout, furnishings—and we decided to go there after dinner.

Before I hopped in a cab and headed to the airport, we said goodbye and she spontaneously said, "I think you must drive an SUV." That is when she had me. Before we met, she knew nothing about me. She didn't know I studied investment and finance. She thought I was a mechanical engineer. Still, just after the first few hours we spent together, she had a hunch I might drive an SUV, which was absolutely true. She was so smart and sensitive and observant!

As planned, I came to Taipei from Kaohsiung City to see her on May 7, 2000, a week after our first meeting, and we had dinner together. She gave me a gift, a small clock embedded in a model golden airplane with the hands representing the propellers of the plane. "I feel your flying heart," she said. I told myself again, this was it. I needed to win her. She had no prior knowledge that I'd studied aerospace engineering. She just felt it. When we were ready to leave for the two-hour drive in the dark, there was a big problem: Despite Doriya's specificity about the house's features, she had no idea where in Jioufen it was or how to get there!

I was undeterred—when I have a plan, I always execute it. So we took the train to the area, found a taxi stand upon arrival, and asked a driver if there were any nearby bed and breakfasts. It was around midnight, and our only requirement was that it be clean. The driver said yes, a friend had a very nice place located a little bit off the main street but with a gorgeous view, so we agreed to go there.

Lo and behold: It was the house with the big windows overlooking the cliff to the harbor that Doriya remembered so well. We were both shocked and speechless.

It was our destiny to be together! As I write these pages, we have been married for over twenty years. And she has always been my counsel and consort and someone I can rely on. I am eternally indebted to her for my career, my life, and my two beautiful and wonderful children.

FOR BETTER OR FOR WORSE

I have always been grateful that Doriya stuck by me when I was going through hell. I confided in her all the details about what was happening with my work and family. She understood and accepted me for who I was. (This attribute was mostly lacking in the women I met during my undergraduate and graduate school days.)

Doriya came to my parents' home for dinner later in 2000, and my father was displeased. He expected me to date and marry a traditional Taiwanese girl who would be polite, obedient, and do domestic chores. However, he never admonished me directly—he probably thought if I didn't marry this woman, I'd be a bachelor my entire life. And it certainly wasn't my father's style to communicate openly—he never expressed his feelings with anything other than "the look."

Doriya faced her family's displeasure, too. It wasn't easy for her to insist to her parents that she would marry me even without their approval; they thought it was crazy for her to wed someone in deep debt without any prospects for making money.

My estrangement from my family has persisted throughout my career. Even though my mother always sided with my father, I harbor no ill will toward her. Our family gatherings for birthdays, the Chinese New Year, and other occasions are polite events. I attend dutifully, but my relatives ignore me. Despite their animosity toward me, I support my relatives financially even today.

My relationship with my father was painful, but I am reconciled to how things transpired. There was an impermeable barrier between us—maybe our conflicts were the result of traditional Taiwanese cultural norms or generational differences, or maybe they were a function of his personality. Regardless, I am at peace with the situation.

My attitude might puzzle some Americans, but remember, I was born Taiwanese Chinese. I maintain the mentality that my parents gave me my life, they gave me the opportunity to study in the US, and they gave me the lessons to be who I am today. I am responsible for paying them back. I am reconciled with myself and have no regrets.

Doriya stuck with me even when we were apart for months or years—me in Hong Kong, she in Kaohsiung,

Taiwan. We married in January 2004, four years after we'd first shared seafood pasta.

MY PRIDE AND JOYS

I'd be woefully remiss if I didn't tell you more about my beloved family before I continue describing my business journey.

Typically, Chinese wedding ceremonies don't include elaborate rituals. They are staid events where the elders give speeches and lunch is served. But Doriya and I had three wedding receptions (yes, three!), and our third reception was a real party.

Two events were held in Kaohsiung City, my hometown—one for Doriya's family and one for mine. Doriya's father was a businessman and had a lot of relatives. My family's reception was smaller and more formal. Doriya and I had to go around to each table of ten and individually toast every one of the guests.

During both family events, we had to behave our best. However, we went wild with our friends in Taipei at the third reception, with wine flowing and an open buffet in a restaurant seating forty. That night we ran out of food because more than *eighty* people showed up. This kind of celebration is typical in the Western world, but it most certainly was not the norm in Taiwan twenty-one years ago! We had such fun, and our friends still talk about that night!

Our first daughter, Celine, was a honeymoon baby born in October 2004. When she arrived, Celine was the only light during the very dark time when we were so poor I had worried about affording baby formula and considered getting back my library card deposit to pay for it. Fortunately, my maternal aunt had a business that provided consumer goods to a chain supermarket. She gave us boxes of sample diapers intended for the store. Doriya and I are eternally grateful for her generosity. The timing of Irene's birth, June 2007, was luckier. By then, my career was slowly on an upward trajectory, and I had some cash reserves; at least I could afford diapers and baby food.

We put a lot of thought into naming our girls. We chose Celine in honor of my favorite romance movie trilogy, *Before Sunrise* (1995). The beautiful actress Julie Delpy played the main character, Celine, who was smart, strong, and pretty. So, it was an aspirational name; and our hopes have been realized! There is an additional significance: In French and Greek, *Celine* means "sky" or "moon."

As I mentioned earlier, Irene's name also has its roots in cinema. You may remember that when I was studying at Pace in New York, a poster of Irène Jacob had a prominent place on my apartment wall. She was the beautiful star of *Three Colors: Red* (1994), which was part of another movie trilogy. The etymology of her name is also aspirational; in Greek, *Irene* means "peace," and

I believe that Irene indeed feels a sense of security and inner well-being.

I hoped to be the kind of father I wished I'd had—someone who respected their children, treated them with love and kindness, and gave them the freedom to make their own choices. I also strove to instill my sense of ethics and values, a love of learning, and an appreciation of books, and cinema, and travel.

We gave Celine and Irene each an iMac minicomputer when they were in first grade, and we didn't place any parental controls on internet use. This was something most Taiwanese thought was crazy and inappropriate. But we taught the girls that computers are tools, and just like knives they have both safe and dangerous uses. We emphasized that we expected them to use the computers properly. They never violated our standards or expectations.

Celine and Irene have adopted my love of reading; their bookcases are overfull. They share my passion for the arts and theater and are very talented singers, famous for performing duets. We took them to my favorite Broadway show in New York, *Les Misérables*, when they were nine and seven years old. Ten days later, they could sing all the songs by memory—like me! Additionally, we enrolled them in an American school in Kaohsiung, the Morrison Academy. Tuition was expensive and became a heavy burden when our finances were low. But education was our priority, so we scrimped on other things.

Our daughters have always been precocious—baking cookies at seven years old and skiing at age four in Japan (there's no snow in Taiwan). They excel at whatever they undertake, and we are very proud of both.

I hope now you will understand why my move to Hong Kong was a bittersweet one. Running my first hedge fund *and* running back and forth between Hong Kong and Taiwan was necessary to ensure my family's future. Soon I would be back on track to succeed in a finance career and to raise our own family in the ways Doriya and I saw fit.

7

Hong Kong: Target Practice and Aiming for the Sun

I certainly wasn't the international traveler in 2003 that I am today, but I had lived in several different places: my parents' house (and briefly, a boarding school) in Kaohsiung, apartments in Wichita and New Jersey, back to my parents' house and a small apartment nearby, and then Taipei. None of these places were in the slightest way fancy.

In September 2003, one year before Celine was born, a new job opportunity took me back and forth between two islands: Taiwan and Hong Kong. I began working for Global Investment Advisors (GIA), a Taiwanese-owned company based in Hong Kong. I advised corporations and high-net-worth individuals on wealth planning and global investing. I educated these clients on data and tax planning, various investment vehicles and funds, and other financial matters. In the process, I acquired knowledge that I apply today to my own personal finances and family legacy planning.

GETTING SETTLED

Although I worked in Hong Kong, I didn't establish a permanent residence there. At first, I stayed at very cheap hotels, from which I came and went, until my home *was* a hotel room. You see, a few years later, a different firm provided me with a housing allowance that would cover an apartment rental. I figured signing a long-stay hotel contract with Courtyard Hong Kong cost almost the same as the housing allowance. The hotel's conveniences made the decision of where to live easy; at the Courtyard, I didn't have to worry about housekeeping, maintenance, and internet, and they even provided breakfast and dinner since I had earned lifetime Marriott Titanium status. So, I signed a four-year contract to stay there. The general manager even threw a rooftop BBQ party for us long-term guests and regulars.

I didn't spend much time in my room anyway. I traveled back and forth between Hong Kong and Taiwan at least once a week. Even after my children were born, my wife and daughters stayed in Taiwan. Still, my family was my priority, and I adapted to the demanding travel and work schedule.

I didn't want my daughters to grow up not knowing me—quite the contrary, I wanted to be close with them. I had learned the painful effects of parental indifference and, even worse, disappointment and disdain. So, I vowed from the beginning that I would share my feelings and communicate openly with my girls. (To this day, our relationships are more like that of equal friends, not like a senior authority to an obedient underling.)

Our lifestyle—with Doriya and the girls in one place and me in another at times—was obviously not very common in Taiwan. But I was forced to start new ventures in Hong Kong because of my difficult financial circumstances at home. As it happened, Doriya, my daughters, and I not only got used to this kind of lifestyle; we actually enjoyed it. It was the beginning of us getting passports and residencies and becoming global citizens. Now, we are comfortable being anywhere in the world and don't feel as if any place is strange to us.

In 2005, after spending two years working for Global Investment Advisors, I left to start my own advisory firm. A consultancy business doesn't require start-up capital; the only overhead was literally my brain (and my time). This was the easiest and quickest way to start my own venture, and it was my first foray into entrepreneurship.

EXTERNAL ASSET MANAGER

Although I only had a small client base, my advisory firm served as a useful networking tool. In 2006, one year before Irene was born, Target Capital Management approached me, looking for help to set up a hedge fund. Target didn't have the knowledge and tools to do so; what they did have were lots of private clients who had lots of money.

I joined Target part-time as a responsible officer (RO), and a director. The Security and Futures Commission (SFC) in Hong Kong—the equivalent of the Securities and Exchange Commission (SEC) in the US—requires that a securities firm have at least two licensed principals to maintain their license to serve on regulated activities, and these principals are called ROs. I became the RO and director and helped Target create their (and my) first hedge fund, trading in commodity futures.

Specifically, my role was to set up an External Asset Management (EAM) business for Target. EAM was a new model at the time, but now it is a mature and widely used institutional investment structure. The concept of EAMs is based on mutually beneficial symbiotic relationships; I developed cooperative partnerships and signed contracts with major banks that have a worldwide presence, including UBS Credit Suisse, Morgan Stanley, and Merrill Lynch.

The advantage of this arrangement for us was that we didn't have to go out to find products or platforms ourselves; instead, we could use what the bank had already spent millions of dollars to develop. At our disposal were sophisticated platforms with a variety of instruments—mutual funds, bonds, stocks, commodities, insurance, and so on. The EAM would recommend to their clients that they open an account with one of these banks. Then, we'd manage their accounts using the banks as custodians.

As you can see, we gave the banks something valuable they did not have—our investors. No matter what the banks charged the clients, the banks shared with us one-half of their earnings, including management fees, advisory fees, and even interest. We split that fifty-fifty with the banks. And Target further split with the advisors. It was a win-win for everyone.

I first had the idea to work with Merrill Lynch and sell the fund for Target, calling it the Merrill Lynch Target Commodity Trading Fund. Merrill Lynch came up with the index and we followed it. It was easy; we did not do stocks, bonds, or commodity analyses or manage trading activity; we just followed the leader, so to speak.

Commodities were our bread and butter. For example, in 2007 when we launched the fund, the world needed precious metals, so they became a valuable commodity to trade. Although the Baltic Shipping Index

(BSI) was very volatile, precious metals were doing well at that moment and were on an upward swing. So the hedge fund invested in them for three years, and the return was outstanding for both the fund and Target's investors.

As I said, the Merrill Lynch Target Commodity Trading Fund was the first fund I set up by myself. The truth is, I had no idea that commodities—in this case, precious metals—would perform so well! I was happy and so were the investors. But if you asked me how I did it, I would say it was pure luck.

THE CRASH: STRUGGLING TO GET CLIENTS AND CASH

During this time, I was certainly earning more money than I had in Taiwan, but my income still was not great. With index funds, you can't charge high management fees, and, as I've explained, we split those low fees with the salespeople who brought the investors on board. On the bright side, at least my income was no longer reduced by two-thirds because in Hong Kong, the Taiwanese government couldn't garnish a portion of my paycheck. I was also benefitting psychologically, as it was satisfying that my work was valued, even though a downside was that I didn't spend 100 percent of my time with my young family.

Still, business was good . . . until it wasn't. In 2008 and 2009, the whole world's financial markets collapsed. The breadth and depth of the situation was beyond imagination. I was still with Target and sat on the board of the University Fund of Kaohsiung University in Taiwan. But it was a very tough time for everyone.

Nevertheless, my advisory business was quite busy, partly because of the economic downturn. Companies needed to find creative ways to survive, and many turned to me for advice. I accepted several project-based consultancy jobs—my background and experience in corporate finance made me a desirable advisor. My reputation was good, and I knew how to put together attractive business plans, fundraise, and restructure companies.

I still wasn't making a lot of money. My clients didn't pay me a retainer fee or an hourly rate; instead, they gave me a success fee. If I hit the target (pun intended) and raised the amount of money they wanted, I'd get paid. Or if I designed an M&A structure and successfully negotiated the terms, I was compensated a small percentage.

It can take six to twelve months to complete one job, and I'd have to wait to get paid. This arrangement is called a zero-sum game—if you don't get paid in three years, and then you get paid, you are good for three years. Essentially, my only compensation was a success fee, dependent on a deal closing.

THE LANTERN'S LIGHT AHEAD

My future was uncertain, but I never lost hope. I always saw a great lantern deep in the night, and I reached for it. I didn't know if I would ever get there, but the lantern kept me going. It didn't have to be a golden light; a shiny, silver (pun intended) beam would suffice. Let me explain why.

By now, you understand that the etymology and meaning of words and names are significant to me. When asked where my first name comes from, I usually give a short version. My answer is: Silver derives from the colorful and smart character Long John Silver, in Robert Louis Stevenson's *Treasure Island.* (You can probably picture him as the epitome of a powerful pirate, with a parrot named Captain Flint on his shoulder.)[5]

But when someone gets to know me better, I offer a longer alternative explanation: Silver represents the "Number Two" philosophy I've followed my entire life. No one ever thought I was any good—not good enough at anything or for anyone—beginning in high school or maybe even before then. Consequently, I decided to strive for "good enough," and achieving 90 percent out of 100 became my goal. I'd be happy with an A and didn't need an A+. Put another way, I would proudly wear a SILVER medal! In addition, silver is a shiny shade of grey. Given my early life circumstances, a grey life, I would try to shine in my own ways.

TRANSITIONS

Over time, I consulted for a couple of Chinese companies that were doing IPOs in Hong Kong. In 2012, one client wanted to buy a publicly listed company on the Hong Kong Stock Exchange.

I sourced a company for my client and helped him do a reverse takeover (RTO). This term refers to a transaction where a person or entity injects capital into a company and acquires control. It was not an easy task, as RTOs require 75 percent of existing independent shareholders' votes to approve them, meaning no one related to the deal could vote. It took quite a while to complete this restructuring deal, and once it was consummated, my client asked me to serve as CEO for a short time to reorganize the company.

When I accepted the CEO and executive director positions of the listed company, I resigned from all my positions at Target. It was the right thing to do—my license in Target was regulated by the SFC, which also regulates listed companies in Hong Kong. I didn't want there to be any confusion or appearance of impropriety. I worked as CEO for about six months until the company stabilized, and then I moved on.

SOLAR POWER

The Chinese macro economy was not great in 2011, except for their solar panel manufacturing business. Additionally, there were many players in the arena, and I didn't have money to invest or an angle to make significant money.

I started to look around for different opportunities and thought outside the box. I have a talent, a gift, for always being a step or two ahead of market trends, and that talent led me to an opportunity in Campania, in Southern Italy—a region that was rife with Mafia activity. But before I take you to that sun-drenched Mediterranean area to meet the "boss" and his "family," I want to offer some additional background about how I got there.

As a consultant, I counseled the leaders of large companies, including a publicly listed Taiwanese semiconductor company, Panjit, founded in 1986 in my hometown of Kaohsiung. The company has several divisions and subsidiaries, including a primary business in semiconductor products and another listed company manufacturing touchscreen panels for electronics. At the time, Panjit Group's chairman was spinning off another subsidiary company, Aide, to manufacture solar panels. I was advising Aide on getting foreign private equity funds to invest in the company during their pre-IPO round.

Ultimately, the CFO and I decided to establish an investment fund—Hyperion—that I would manage, and that Panjit would be a limited partner in—an investor.

Why was Aide so keen on manufacturing solar panels for the Italian market? Because their government was heavily subsidizing alternative energy.

In fact, government subsidies were the key to China's success in the solar panel manufacturing industry.

Many large solar panel companies, such as First Solar in Canada and SolarWatt in Germany, already existed worldwide. But Chinese companies surpassed the others because of this significant advantage.. Government subsidies enabled them to produce panels cheaply and sell them throughout Europe for half the price of Western manufacturers, who went bankrupt when they couldn't compete.

Essentially, we were trying to create a moat or carve a wall into the fortress China had built around the solar industry. My solution: Enter through Italy!

We wanted to avoid doing business with China because they are often not straightforward. Little did we know that businesspeople in Italy were tricky, too.

HYPERION: THE FATHER OF THE SUN

Finally, here was my lantern; the solar energy industry energized me with light and possibilities! Its electricity bolted me into my new business, Hyperion Capital Management, named for the father of the sun in Greek mythology (the sun being Helios). Hyperion was the Titan god of heavenly light.

This name was another very deliberate choice. What held true for naming my daughters also applied to naming my businesses. I initially considered using an Asian name for my hedge fund but was concerned it would be too difficult to pronounce. So, I again turned to Greek and Roman mythology and realized the names Apollo and Helios were common company names. Thus, Hyperion emerged.

With that bit of history about Hyperion's origins, you are ready to accompany me back in time to Southern Italy, where I had unusual business dealings and encountered and overcame many obstacles. My success and resilience were not merely a matter of getting up and dusting myself off. Being resilient required much more; I needed to build my confidence, solve problems creatively, and identify opportunities that others couldn't see.

To use another expression derived from ancient stories: It took a herculean effort to turn my business visions into profitable realities. It also required the support of others who trusted me and my talent and were willing to invest in them.

8

Southern Italy: An Outsider Doing Business with a Different Kind of Family

There's an old Chinese expression about resilience, 摸著石頭過河, which translates to "crossing the river by touching the stones." This means that you can overcome whatever challenges you face the same way you do when you cross a river and there's no bridge spanning the sides or sense of the depth of the water.

You keep touching whatever stones you can and continue steadily, step-by-step. This is the way you find stability and progress on the other side. This is precisely how I conducted business in Southern Italy. There were many times when no bridge existed, and, even worse, when an unexpected flood engulfed me. So, I used all my brain power, time, and effort to keep my head above water as I felt my way to the other side.

SEEDS OF AN ENTERPRISE

To get Aide up and running, Panjit invested $9 million in seed capital and Hyperion raised money from outside investors. We would build solar power plants in three regions: Campania, a southern region between Rome and Naples; the island of Sardinia; and Piedmont in northwest Italy. Our largest power plant project would be in Campania; we would also build a greenhouse project in Sardinia and four smaller projects in Piedmont.

We formed a special purpose vehicle (SPV)—a separate legal entity created so a subsidiary company could undertake a specific business activity. In our case, that activity was building solar power projects. SPVs are commonly used in structured finance applications such as asset securitization, joint ventures, or property deals; or to isolate parent company assets, operations, or risks. Thus, we combined all our solar energy projects into one subsidiary that I managed.

In any business deal, the first task above all others is to seek tax advisories that will shape the structure of the process. Given that we were foreigners investing in Italy, the withholding tax could have been as high as 25 to

30 percent. I decided to set up an EU holding entity in Rotterdam, the Netherlands, holding shares of our SPVs in Italy.

The plan was to go to Italy, lease the land for twenty-five years, and hire a construction company to complete the projects. However, all three projects ran into serious problems from the beginning.

As it turns out, many engineering, procurement, and construction (EPC) firms in Southern Italy—particularly in the Campania region—are largely controlled by multiple Mafia families. So, to get any construction done, you have often to deal with these no-good thugs. (Please excuse my harsh characterization, but that was my experience.)

When we began taking bids for the work, we thought we were dealing with several different companies bidding against one another . . . but in reality, there was effectively only one local EPC company. All these apparently independent companies were linked to one another via back channels; beneath the façade they were apparently just a single organization led by one or more dons, all of whom adhered to a strict hierarchy and an inviolable code. Their culture and mode of doing business were literally foreign to me!

When the time came to sign the EPC contract, our terms, of course, stated that the construction company must buy the solar panels necessary to complete the projects from our company. After all, why would a solar panel manufacturer use another manufacturer's panels on their own buildings?! But they balked at that and insisted on using third-party providers—their own people.

AN UNUSUAL MEETING IN THE CAMPANIA REGION

Dealing with Italians is a lot like dealing with the mainland Chinese: They don't trust anybody. They insisted on a contract—in Italian—that defined an incredible array of minuscule details. This demand was very different from how deals and contracts were structured in Hong Kong, where I work.

Hong Kong was then governed by common law developed during British colonization, under which it is not necessary to define *everything* in your contract agreement. If a dispute arises in the future, then you negotiate a solution; if that fails, the courts have case law to fall back on for guidance. But in Italy, they don't believe in case law. You must define every single detail of every possible eventuality, however unlikely. And yet things can still easily go wrong.

After ten days of negotiating in Bari, Puglia, for the Campanian project, we still couldn't reach an agreement. They were all very stubborn, and sometimes they acted very angry. Then, one day, one of their people called me and said, "Hey, we don't have a meeting today. Let's take a ride. I'd like you to meet someone." Carlos showed up at my door, and we drove an hour and a half to Potenza, the capital of Basilicata, a region bordering Campania.

I had no idea where we were going. Throughout the drive I just thought, *This is very beautiful scenery.* Our destination turned out to be a town near Potenza called Matera. When we arrived, the first thing I noticed was an impressive, heavy motorcycle parked in front of the house.

I was introduced to the person they wanted me to meet. He was in his fifties, very warm and friendly, and we sat down for a cup of coffee. I admired the collection of old clocks on his office wall—thirty or forty of them from all over the world. They all appeared to be in working condition, but not all the clocks had the correct time. Maybe they were set to show different time zones; I don't know.

He asked me how I was doing and where I was from, and we just chatted and made small talk. I asked if the motorcycle in front of the house was his, and he confirmed it was. He asked me if I'd seen the movie *The Passion of the Christ.* I said yes, I had, and he said, "It was shot right here in Matera!" It was all very cordial.

Throughout the meeting, I had a strong feeling: *I am not meeting an ordinary person.* But I was not afraid, not for one moment at any point during my visit. Perhaps it was stupid or naïve not to fear this man, but I didn't. He was quite charming. He was like a very kind elder.

So far, my impressions from the day were of a beautiful remote area, a massive motorcycle, a large collection of clocks, strong coffee, and a friendly gentleman.

We didn't talk about business at all. I think he was just trying to get to know me, to understand my character. I was being tested so he could decide whether he liked me. (I wonder what would have happened if he didn't!) Our meeting lasted forty minutes, and afterward, I was driven back to Bari. The next day, we signed the deal with no further problems . . . at least not for a while. That was when it hit me: I was actually meeting the Don, their Godfather.

CAMPANIA AND PIEDMONT

The power plant project didn't start off very well. I had to extend a bridge loan of 4 million euros from Hyperion to the project because there were so many local problems, and we couldn't get the power plant online as scheduled. When the plant was finally connected, I was unable to recoup my loan. So, I transferred all the rights to the power plant from Hyperion to Aide because they had the resources to complete the project; they've owned the power plant since 2011. Turns out, it was a very good result after all. Aide is still enjoying the monthly income generated from the power plant today.

Unfortunately, the €4 million I spent on the Campania project affected the one we'd started in Piedmont; without being able to recoup the loan, Hyperion didn't have enough money to pay for the construction already underway. The Italians needed to pay their workers.

They threatened to take legal action against the fund as an investor if they didn't get paid within a week. The Mafia, with its multiple dons, was a looming presence. I spent a lot of time explaining the situation to them, but they were not happy.

I wasn't happy either, to put it mildly, and I couldn't sleep.

Nor could I let go of the project. I just couldn't let it fail, even though as the fund manager, I wasn't personally responsible. In theory, I could have just told the investors it hadn't worked out—that I was sorry for their loss. After all, that's how life is. Even Hyperion's biggest limited partner, Panjit, was willing to forfeit the project.

But I couldn't move on. I could not accept failure.

As I said, I put together all the cash Hyperion had at the time—around 4 million euros—and injected it into the project. What I haven't yet mentioned is that the money was a no-strings-attached, interest-free loan.

Most of the investors did not know that to resuscitate the project, I had put my own money into Hyperion without any interest. They didn't know I single-handedly prevented a major loss for them, enabling them to profit eventually. I wasn't supposed to do so, nor I was I required to. Yet I did.

However, Panjit, the seeding company, was aware of the actions I took to save the company, and they were very grateful. As I see it, being a businessman with integrity matters. Being a man who doesn't accept defeat and instead solves problems matters to me personally and professionally. I've learned that these qualities matter to others, too.

It's like karma; when you do something good for people, people will do something good for you.

Panjit's appreciation and goodwill led to their providing significant seed money for my next venture, Siegfried Capital Partners. While they had invested $9 million in Hyperion, their initial investment in Siegfried was much higher: $30 million. And their continued investment to date totals $150 million. Siegfried is now a $3 billion, AUM-managed company, but without Panjit's start-up funds there is no way it would have become so successful. But more on that later.

SARDINIA . . . AND MILAN

At the same time as we were contending with the Campania and Piedmont challenges, our other venture in Sardinia was going badly, too. We found that the people there are also often quite tricky—a traditional Chinese way of saying they are sneaky, dishonest, and untrustworthy. They won't even shake your hand.

The Sardinians knew we were outsiders who were unfamiliar with their culture, laws, and "how things are done." They tried to convince us that the way they conducted business was typical in their country, and there was no wiggle room.

As an Asian man, I was deemed a particularly untrustworthy outsider.

Arguing with Southern Italians is very difficult. We didn't really understand their behavior and couldn't predict the outcome of any potential problems that might arise. But we just had a bad feeling. We had a lawyer, but he was from the northern part of the country, near the Austrian border, so he wasn't well-versed in how to deal with Sardinians either.

The Sardinians insisted that the contracts all be written in Italian and that the ruling court be in Cagliari, Sardinia. We said no, everything must be in English, and the court must be in Milan, which has a solid business infrastructure attracting many foreign businesses. I insisted on it.

Negotiations went on for many days before we finally wore the Sardinians down, and they signed the agreement. But that agreement didn't last—they wanted to back out. So, we filed a lawsuit against them—and won. It was a good thing I insisted that the court be in Milan because if it had been in Caliari, we would have lost for sure. All the people we were negotiating with were cozy with the judges there.

The deal collapsed. But at least the firm didn't lose any money on it.

THE CAYMAN ISLANDS

When people hear you're doing business or opening bank accounts in the Cayman Islands, their first thought is usually, *Oh, they're up to no good—probably laundering money.*

European countries, especially Italy, do not like dealing with Cayman companies because of this misapprehension. But that's exactly what it is—a misapprehension!

Before setting up a holding company in the Netherlands, Hyperion established its business in the Cayman Islands for tax purposes. I structured Hyperion as follows: a Taiwanese company investing in a Cayman fund that invests in a Dutch company that invests in an Italian company. It's all perfectly aboveboard and legal.

For this reason, when Hyperion was doing business in Italy, we had to convince them that we were from Taiwan. And that set off another challenge: They have a one-China policy, meaning they view the People's Republic of China as the sole legal government of China; they do not recognize Taiwan as a sovereign state with its own democratically elected government. This, in addition to their insistence that agreements be drawn up in Italian without a parallel English translation, made dealing with them quite frustrating.

As if that wasn't challenging enough, when I finally went to sign the agreement, I was asked to prove that

I had the power to do so. I needed to draft a formal letter, sign it in the presence of a notary, and then have it apostilled by the Italian consulate in Taiwan. But the consulate there said they couldn't verify my identity or certify my signature because their exclusive function was to certify Italian people in Taiwan or a Taiwanese company in Italy. They would not certify a Taiwanese company elsewhere, especially one in the Cayman Islands.

We kept going around and around in circles. Then, I finally came up with an innovative solution: I would jump out of the Taiwan box and leverage Hong Kong's status. Taiwan is not a member of the Hague, the international court in the Netherlands, but Hong Kong is!

INTERNATIONAL DEALMAKING

I met many challenges doing business in Italy. But, as my favorite guiding saying goes, I crossed the river by touching the stones step-by-step and learning important lessons along the way. I was able to find solutions to a set of serious problems and obstacles, whether by insisting on bilingual contracts or resolving disputes in Milan or the Hague.

The possibility of interacting with the Mafia seemed to be constant in Italy, but I wasn't afraid. In the years since then, I have had to deal with strange or dangerous, crazy people many times, and they don't deter me. If I hadn't had this experience in Italy, I might have been more intimidated when negotiating deals. But I am prepared to stand my ground.

The experiences in Italy also prepared me to deal with people from different cultures objectively and sympathetically—to think more from their perspective whenever possible. It's likely that adapting to American culture while studying at US universities was instrumental in my development—not just academically but also personally.

My family and I still love Italy, and we visit all the time. I enjoy the food and wine, especially in Piedmont, two hours south of Turin. But after those experiences, I have never returned to the southern part of the country. Most of my work since then has been in Northern Italy. It is much nicer there in the sense of business environment! Nevertheless, I would still like to visit beautiful places in Southern Italy. I'd love to see Matera again and Sicily, too. I sometimes imagine myself walking amid Sicilian farmlands, like Al Pacino in *The Godfather* (1972).

BEAUTIFUL FRIENDSHIPS IN ITALY

My Italian adventure didn't end without rewards. Despite the setbacks of running a business there, I met some of the best Italians: Fabrizio, Piernicola, Massimo, and others.

Fabrizio is a big boy. He has run various companies in different industries over the years, including telecom, solar plant construction, and juice making. He has a good heart and lives in Turin with his beautiful Ukrainian wife. One thing we love about Fabrizio is that he is a huge foodie. No matter where he takes us and no matter what we eat or drink, it is always the best of everything. You can see the finest virtues of an Italian in him.

Piernicola is a fourth-generation winemaker. Soon his daughter will become the fifth generation. He owns a boutique vineyard and winery in the beautiful countryside of Nieve, just a ten-minute drive to d'Alba in my favorite wine region of Piedmont. Pier is the reason why we fell in love with Italian wines. When you enter Taiwan, you can only bring two bottles of wine without declaring. So, to be able to drink more of Pier's wines, we applied and got approved for an alcohol-importing permit. Pier is also a big boy who loves playing electric guitars. When we visited, he took us to the wine bank, showing off his impressive collection. One of his wines has earned a place on the list of top 100 Italian wines. The wine bank preserves the vineyard and winery's best vintages of their Barbaresco and the soil that produced it.

Massimo is a totally different Italian. He was born and grew up in South Tyrol, where the first language is German. (Northern Italy was under Austrian rule for hundreds of years.) Massimo is my lawyer in Italy and can speak fluent German, Italian, French, English, and some Chinese. I attended his wedding to his beautiful wife at his father-in-law's castle in South Tyrol. During the reception dinner, which was opulently set up on a big lawn between the Alpines, I met more German-speaking Italian friends.

Massimo's wife and father-in-law are very special. I didn't know why at the wedding everybody went to greet him and shake his hand until I saw a big poster on a local bus; his father-in-law, Reinhold Messner, is Italy's most famous mountaineer, author of eighty published books, and the first person in the world to climb Mount Everest and all fourteen mountains over eight thousand meters high without supplementary oxygen. Massimo's wife manages Messner's five museums, which display all the discoveries and history of Reinhold's legends.

EXIT STRATEGY: ON TO THE NEXT VENTURE

When Hyperion was initially established in 2011, I felt like I had been thrown into a river without knowing how to swim. Honestly, I didn't have enough experience running a private equity fund for greenfield projects in solar power plants—and certainly not enough to do business in a foreign country! I was not just running a fund; I was dealing as an outsider in insular communities with different ways of conducting business. Because I didn't know all the rules, I was learning by doing.

The plan was for the hedge fund to be terminated in five years, with an option for me, as the manager, to extend it for up to two more years. But I didn't want to wait seven years until 2018, so I started reaching out early to local people and other hedge funds about buying the power plants from Hyperion. This allowed everyone to do their due diligence and negotiate the terms.

I would soon move on to my next exciting endeavor: Siegfried Capital, the investment management group of which I'm the founder, chairman, and CIO. A company that has a presence in Hong Kong, Luxembourg, and the Cayman Islands. It's fair to say that my dealings managing a hedge fund in Italy, and the support Panjit extended to me, were pivotal in launching this next phase of my career.

9

Luxembourg: Creating The Siegfried Fund

As you know by now, nothing has ever come easy for me. I've had to figure out wholly original solutions to surmount overwhelming obstacles. That is, I have slain many dragons.

My list of conquests includes both big and small successes: Leaving an unhappy family home. Going from an abysmal academic record to earning dual US university degrees. Rising above poverty with a heavy yoke of inherited debt around my neck. Finding new part-time professor positions after multiple unfair firings. Observing unsavory stock-price manipulations. Pivoting after a merger threatened my investment banking job. Returning home when no good job alternatives presented themselves. Surviving in a country (Taiwan) where the environmental and political winds were constantly shifting. Working at my father's company on an IPO aborted by government policies, leading to bankruptcy. And running my first private equity fund in Italy, where the culture and business laws were stacked against me.

I was clearly ready to try something new and exciting. If it meant slaying another dragon, I would be ready for that, too.

My next venture, Siegfried Capital, would be a resounding success. As I alluded to earlier, it grew from \$30 million of seed capital to a company listed on the Luxembourg Stock Exchange with around \$3.1 billion in assets under management (AUM). But developing this fund was not without a lot of wrangling and fire-breathing, as you will soon see.

WHAT'S IN A NAME?

When I decided to start a hedge fund after Hyperion had run its course, the name Siegfried seemed an appropriate choice. I've already described how I deeply considered meaningful names—influenced by the arts—for my daughters and companies. Siegfried Capital's name was no exception.

The Old Norse and Germanic myth of Siegfried centers around a courageous hero who kills a threatening dragon and then bathes in its blood to prevent further danger. The German name translates literally to "victory." As an opera fan, I was also mindful of Richard Wagner's epic German opera *Der Ring des Nibelungen*, in which *Siegfried* is one of four parts of its cycle.

I considered other powerful Norse names, like Thor and Fred, but Siegfried naturally emerged as the victor. The name is catchy—not too familiar, yet not too strange. It seemed perfect to me.

When I had my first exploratory meetings about the new fund with people in Zurich, Switzerland, I was repeatedly asked why I chose the name; apparently, it is popular because I've since met a dozen people named Siegfried in Switzerland and Germany!

THE CONTEXT AND CONCEPT

The idea for the Siegfried Capital fund was an outgrowth of many conversations I'd had with economist Dr. Typhoon Wen, my university colleague and fellow professor in the Department of Finance in Kaohsiung National University of Applied Science. Dr. Wen specialized in economics and trade finance. In 2003, while I was teaching investment banking and portfolio management, he taught supply chain finance—a type of financing for businesses buying goods wherein a third-party financial institution provides funding to the buyer's suppliers, based on the buyer's creditworthiness. Dr Wen was highly experienced and instrumental in conceptualizing the formation of my company.

In 1998, Dr. Wen established VTeam Financial Services Group, which became a leader in supply chain financing in Greater China. When we began brainstorming ideas for how to work together, his company was very small. Its initial mission was to design IT software for banks and sell, install, and train its users. In 2014, the Japanese venture capital company SoftBank saw the software's potential and not only invested but also advised Dr. Wen to expand from IT to become a factoring platform, streamlining the entire invoicing process.

VTeam expanded rapidly—today, 95 percent of Taiwanese banks and 65 percent of Chinese national banks use this software.[6] It was a unicorn company, an exchange marketplace for supply chain financing.

Factoring receivables has been a standard business practice in the US since the 1960s. (Historically, it has been a mode of financing since the 1800s or even earlier.) However, twenty years ago, such financing was very new in Taiwan and unknown in China. I was among those who had no clue that there were private companies in the US and elsewhere whose business model was factoring receivables.

Years ago, a seller in China had to be backed by a bank. If Walmart or another company came to China to make a purchase—say, of clothes, shoes, or pencils—they would issue a letter of credit (LC), stipulating the bank would release the money to the seller upon delivery of the goods. But it no longer works this way.

Now, the trade finance process goes like this: Let's say a company sells boxes of shoes to Walmart, there are agreed-upon payment terms; it could be 90 days, 180 days, etc. Once the shoes are delivered, it is Walmart's account payable and the seller's account receivable. The seller doesn't get paid until the maturity date in the payment terms.

But sellers don't want to wait for their money! They need money to pay for their overhead and employees. They could also use the cash to manufacture more goods and sell them to someone else.

So, how can companies get their payments sooner?

They can take their account receivables (A/Rs) to the bank as collateral for a loan. The catch is that large Chinese banks like Bank of China, Bank of Construction, and China Merchant Bank only want to lend money to large corporations or state-owned enterprises (SOEs). These companies are considered safe bets that can quickly disclose required financial information and fulfill their obligations.

Since China's traditional credit system disfavored small- to medium-sized enterprises (SMEs), smaller companies had to obtain much-needed capital in other ways to survive and perhaps thrive.

FROM SHADOW BANKING TO FACTORING PLATFORMS

In 2010, the shadow banking industry in China exploded. This term refers to private lenders (sometimes loan sharks) who operate outside traditional channels and are not subject to strict regulatory requirements. SMEs are often so desperate for funds that they are willing to pay high borrowing rates, often 15 to 18 percent, to such lenders.

When Dr. Wen shifted VTeam's business from IT to a private trading platform, it still wasn't easy for vendors or suppliers (medium or small) to get bank loans. To join this trading marketplace, a company had to be registered and provide its financials for due diligence scrutiny. It was initially very selective—only 8 percent of applicants were accepted. The trading platform gradually became more desirable to Asian banks because the assets were vetted, and the risks were minimized.

Dr. Wen's business model constantly evolved, and we continued to talk. The trades on VTeam's platform were primarily among Chinese companies because China maintains strict capital control. It was very difficult—if not impossible—for money to go in and come out.

China tightly controls *every* transaction, even among friends. For example, let's say your neighbor desperately needs $10,000. They ask you if they could borrow the money from you, and you agree. They thank you and say they will repay you with interest.

Although the law is not often enforced, you don't want to take that chance: This transaction is illegal in China! Why? Because China requires private lending licenses. They also now issue factoring licenses. And every province issues its *own* factoring license! The consequences of not adhering to the government's laws are severe.

When the concept of A/R factoring—buying and selling obligations—entered the picture in about 2015, there was so much I didn't know. I could have easily violated laws because I never knew they existed.

TESTING THE INTERNATIONAL WATERS

In 2015, while living in Hong Kong, I finally saw my opportunity in this arena and founded Siegfried Capital offshore to trade outside the channel—outside the typical technical indicators. The investment account receivables were in domestic China, so I tried to raise capital outside of China to invest worldwide. It didn't work out. I tried again in 2016, convinced I could navigate this *blue* ocean where I faced very little competition. I would take the time and design a structure that worked.

Siegfried took advantage of the opportunity to revamp its model when Chinese companies began selling goods to the Western world in earnest and flooded the foreign market. (China became the world's largest exporter in 2009.[7]) Now, many countries, including the US, Europe, and Japan, are coming to China to buy goods.

I recognized that international trades are essential for global economic growth and factoring, and that A/R finance is the rising new asset class to support international trade.

Siegfried's global asset management's business eventually grew to 255 buyers, many of which are big names like Walmart, Amazon, Home Depot, and Target. We no longer needed to worry about Chinese capital restrictions because we bought receivables and got paid outside of China. Business became much easier.

But this growth did not happen overnight, so let me flash back to Siegfried Capital's early days.

I was still a novice—there were many technical details I didn't understand, and it took me many years to master them. (I felt almost as naïve as I had when I started in my first securities job, the investment bank in Taipei, back in 1999.) Nevertheless, I tried to focus on what I knew well and had the mental agility and logical thinking skills to fill in my knowledge gaps. I had matured and developed more confidence. So, I focused on designing my fund properly. But even so, I didn't know if my venture would work out.

I started to build up funds in 2017 and launched a pilot project in 2018. As I described in the previous chapter, Panjit, the Taiwanese semiconductor giant, seeded the company with $30 million. Their investment was a great show of appreciation for my work saving its business in Italy; it was also proof that this model works and is accepted by a regulated institutional investor.

I now had a story to sell: *Hey, this famous Taiwanese stock-listed company invested in Siegfried Capital!* Other investors followed, including friends and family, and I raised $43 million in two to three months.

This pilot fund was a very important springboard for Siegfried. We designed it to last three years; nobody could come in or go out within that period. But to cover all possibilities, I got the fund listed on the Luxembourg Stock Exchange (LSE) in case anyone didn't want to wait three years to sell their shares on the LSE. It was a successful endeavor. During the three-year period, not a single investor wanted out. When we terminated the fund, we gave our investors a choice: get paid immediately or transfer their shares into Siegfried's second financing round. Most decided to roll their investment into the second fund.

THE PATH TO A PUBLICLY TRADED FUND

My strategic philosophy is that in business (and in life), you don't need to know everything from the beginning. Instead, you must take your first step—touch that first stone—and the right path will become clearer and clearer. You just have to get started.

This thinking led to Siegfried's success, but first, I had to constantly pivot and explain my thinking to others. No one understood my analyses or the concept and potential of factoring receivables. I had to learn by doing and then teach others how I'd done it!

The first fund was relatively easy to manage because it was a private and closed-end fund; I didn't need any regulatory body's approval. Still, I was simultaneously working to establish a publicly traded collective fund. I had no clue about how to do this, and, as usual, I thought outside the box, consulted some friends, and eventually built a workable model.

Why Europe? In Taiwan, insurance companies were very interested in the factoring business model because it is a low-risk, high-return, short-term loan. However, they aren't able to engage in it because under Taiwan insurance law, insurance companies' investments are restricted and well-defined and don't include non-standardized short-term loans. I was approached by some insurance companies regarding these opportunities in 2014 and decided to set up Siegfried in 2015 because I knew if I could find a way to securitize trade receivables, we could attract large financial institutions to invest in us. I maintained my vision while no one believed me or thought it could work.

Under insurance law in Taiwan, insurance companies' money can be invested in publicly traded stocks, investment-grade bonds, mutual funds with long track records, or private funds with even longer track records of $500 million or more in AUM, while the managers had to be from an Organisation for Economic Co-operation and Development (OECD) country. There are thirty-eight OECD member countries, and China isn't among them. I settled on domiciling the Siegfried fund in Luxembourg.

Why Luxembourg—especially when I was living in Hong Kong? I knew it was an OECD country, and since I had conducted business in Italy, another OECD country whose companies were subjected to strict regulation and compliances, I believed I could manage my way around such regulations again. Also, Luxembourg is the world's second-largest fund management center (second only to the US).[8] It is a politically stable country and the seat of the European Court of Justice, the European Parliament Secretariat, the European Investment Bank, and the European Investment Fund. Luxembourg was a wise choice for Siegfried Capital for many reasons, including a favorable tax system.

But I had to pave Siegfried's road to Luxembourg on my own. From the outset, I had to find the right parties—lawyers, custodians, traders, auditors, administrators, and banks.

I worked closely with UBS, the multinational investment bank, which became the fund's custodian.

Additionally, a friend from the UK, Kenneth Hugues, connected me to a PricewaterhouseCoopers (PwC) lawyer in Luxembourg. PwC became my first legal and tax advisor and audit firm.

We needed to produce a valuation report on a regular basis, which no one else knew how to do. I did. I worked out the calculations, prepared a computer spreadsheet, and explained them to everyone who showed interest. Even PwC, a leading worldwide professional services firm, had to be taught how to properly audit the fund!

Initially, the biggest hurdle was figuring out my business model and investment strategy so I could convince others it was sound. My strategy wasn't fixed—it constantly evolved. As I had done with my first fund, I explained how supply chain financing works and educated all the parties on how the Siegfried fund was structured. (My experience teaching corporate financial engineering at universities served me well.)

Doing this over and over again, day after day, led to many sleepless nights. If I wasn't effective, the fund would fizzle.

I had already made some progress, having decided that the fund would be domiciled in Luxembourg, but there were still many hoops to jump through to make an international public company a reality.

How would I get approved to list Siegfried on the stock exchange? What were the tax implications? What court of law would adjudicate agreements and disputes? How could I make all this happen while I was living in Hong Kong?

Navigating tax issues was also a constant headache. Consider the facts: I run a management company in Hong Kong, and the funds are domiciled in Luxembourg and the Cayman Islands. Trading stocks and bonds is not taxable in Hong Kong. However, trading accounts receivable *is* taxable. We didn't know that. Once we learned about it, we had to change the structure; we didn't want the funds to pay an additional 16.5 percent income tax in Hong Kong, as that would lead to 16.5 percent less profit for the investors.

Fortunately, I figured this out with PwC's tax department's counsels before the launch of the funds. Otherwise, we would have been in big trouble. I was able to modify the fund's structure to comply with the law before the funds debuted.

Siegfried Luxembourg finally became a Société d'investissement à Capital Variable (SICAV) fund, an open-ended investment vehicle offered in Europe. To do so, the approval of the Commission de Surveillance du Secteur Financier (CSSF), the equivalent of the SEC in the US, was required. The instrument would be highly regulated.

It took sixteen months for Siegfried to get CSSF approval! And as of this writing, it's been in business for seven years.

There is more to tell you about my travels and the blood, sweat, and tears that went into establishing Siegfried Capital. And more to say about the friendships, joys, and profits that made it all worthwhile. So, please read on.

10

Europe and Japan: Developing Siegfried Capital

I have felt clueless about so many things in my life—clueless about inherited debt, about how the Taiwanese educational system limited me, about how investment bankers set stock prices in boiler rooms, about how to start a hedge fund, and much more.

My wife, Doriya, and I frequently discuss how surreal our present blessed, comfortable circumstances seem. We have lived in deep, dark holes, yet we crawled out of them again and again by harnessing perseverance and hope.

By taking one step at a time, a path always reveals itself to me—sometimes by happenstance and other times by considerable conscious effort. The important lesson is to get started no matter what.

My sense of naïveté and modesty tell me that my successes are attributable simply to good luck. Still, I am an engineer, a rational guy, and I understand that I have had something to do with my achievements. I have used every idea, every resource—*everything* available to me—as a learning opportunity. Ultimately, I have created a viable, highly profitable, and sustainable investment product.

Doriya and I have prepared for the future with the fear in the back of our minds—based on twenty years of hardship—that something bad might happen. Even though we have amassed generational wealth and set up a family trust fund for the future, we live modestly and debt-free. The most expensive timepiece I've splurged on for myself is a Garmin sports smartwatch that cost $800. (Frankly, I could afford a Patek Philippe.)

I choose to spend my money on spiritual, intellectual, and experiential things. I am thrilled and honored that my wife and I were invited to attend the ninetieth birthday celebration of the Dalai Lama in northern India. Unfortunately, His Holiness was not well during those planned days. Because we didn't want to cancel the trip, we still went to the Himalayas in Rishikesh and I had an unforgettable spiritual week of finding my inner self. I have always loved traveling. (Remember how I would scrape enough together to venture abroad cheaply during college breaks?) I have been fortunate to give my daughters opportunities to see the world, too. Further, I have offered them the closeness, openness, and encouragement that my family denied me during my youth.

It feels right to contemplate these things as I continue the story of the Siegfried funds and how the company's expertise in supply chain financing has garnered a global client base whose portfolios we proudly manage.

WHO TO KNOW, WHAT TO KNOW, AND WHERE TO GO

As I described in the previous chapter, Siegfried Capital was founded after I received inquiries from Taiwanese insurance companies about the factoring business model. They were attracted to the low-risk, high-return, short-term loans; however, I wasn't particularly enthused about working with them—Taiwanese insurance laws were too restrictive to yield a significant return on investment. I turned to a place I was familiar with and had been working in for years: Europe. Despite my bad experience in Italy, I had learned my way around.

I launched Siegfried with sound strategies and trading models, training personnel and obtaining investments from friends and family. Although I was convinced of the viability of supply chain financing, I was still unsure of how to proceed: Would my trading models work? Would investors be interested? Who should I talk to? Where should I go?

I hoped to find a market for my asset management business in Hong Kong, China, and Taiwan. However,

I had learned in Taiwan, and soon discovered in Hong Kong, that Asian institutional investors were speculators looking for double-digit returns. The fact that my fund was stable and low risk was irrelevant to them. There was zero interest in my fund. (US investors have similar high expectations.)

All I knew for sure was that I had to take another step forward!

I felt the Siegfried business venture was my last shot, and I didn't have a plan B.

Here is a perfect example of the confluence of good luck and hard work. In 2018, I went to Zurich to visit some friends. My personal banker was also located there, so I met with her to discuss my ideas and plans for Siegfried. She kindly introduced me to various departments of UBS, and my conversations with them were eye-opening.

Through my Zurich banker's contacts, I gained an understanding of the European financial environment and investors' expectations. My business plan took shape: Focus on Europe! The prevailing interest rate there was -.5 percent at that time. Imagine that: a *negative* interest rate. (That meant if you took out a mortgage in Switzerland, the bank would pay you interest, not vice versa.) So, Siegfried's stable, low-risk, 6 to 7 percent return on investment seemed almost too good to be true to Europeans.

The trip to Zurich to visit friends was pivotal; Europeans clamored to talk with me, whereas investors in

Asia (and the US) had listened momentarily and then quickly turned away.

THE EXPONENTIAL VALUE OF CONNECTIONS

About fifteen years ago, I met a guy from a very wealthy family in Hong Kong named Alan Hung, and we became good friends (and still are). I'm honestly not sure why he was willing to talk to me at all—he was out of my league both socially and economically.

Alan and I got along very well, discussing music, books, history, movies, wines, etc., and had dinner together regularly. We discussed the investment strategy of Siegfried Capital and how to grow it, and I asked him if he would join the company's board of directors; he agreed and is still actively involved with the company.

When I told Alan about my plans to go to Switzerland, he said there was someone special I should meet there. I had no preconceptions when this special someone, let's call him Mr. X, and I got together for a simple pasta dinner, but it was a fortuitous encounter. Mr. X had recently moved back to Switzerland from New York after being laid off from his twenty-year career at Citibank. He was the head of structured financing and had institutional clients, including major banks, insurance companies, and pension funds.

Mr. X is extremely astute and understood what I was trying to achieve with my fund, but that was that . . .

until I spontaneously invited him to join me at my meeting with UBS. (Apparently, I've developed good instincts about people over the years, a trait that has become commonly known as "emotional intelligence" or EQ). At the meeting with UBS, we discussed Siegfried's business strategy and goals, and Mr. X added valuable input. He also had a valuable network of institutional contacts from his many years at Citibank.

Mr. X and I were a good match: I had a good product, and he had a solid client base of investors to sell it to. I didn't yet fully understand how business was conducted in Europe, and he did. By the time I returned to Switzerland in 2019, Mr. X had already elicited much interest in the fund and had planned a road show for me.

Because of all of this evidence of synergy between us, it made sense to sign a deal. Mr. X changed everything for me and my business, and I remain extremely grateful. I recently learned that the feeling was mutual.

ON THE ROAD IN EUROPE

Mr. X and I spent countless days traveling to meet potential investors in Switzerland, the UK, the Netherlands, and Germany. It was a whirlwind of meetings, hotel rooms, and train rides, not a sightseeing trip. After daylong meetings, everyone was tired and went their separate ways. In Asian culture, it is traditional to socialize and relax over dinner and drinks at the close of business, but European culture was different.

The road trip was all business, and it seemed like we talked to everyone! I probably repeated the same speech to thirty different groups yet gained insights and feedback each time. My partners and I became better equipped to improvise based on the audience.

I particularly like the Chinese saying 教學相長, which translates literally to "learning while teaching." I've had that marvelous experience most of my life—certainly when I was Corinna's study partner and tutor in my master of science in finance program at Pace, when I held part-time professor positions at universities in Kaohsiung, then as I parented my daughters, and while explaining my business models and the concept of supply chain investing to potential European investors.

I learned that investors might appear extremely enthusiastic when meeting face-to-face and exchanging ideas, but that excitement can quickly fade. The people I met in Europe were initially excited about the significant contrast between the rate of return I promised—5 to 6 percent—and the negative interest they accrued in their bank deposits, where they paid fees. I explained data demonstrating how our funds achieve that rate of return as well as the low risk they carry.

But the supply chain financing asset class was still too new to them. At the time, Siegfried only had a few million dollars of AUM, and institutional investors looked for $300 million AUM with a three-year track record of success. This presented us with a significant hurdle. But we persevered and eventually reached and surpassed those benchmarks.

When I returned home from the long European trip, I was somewhat disappointed that those potential investors hadn't materialized. Their interest seemed very promising. But the trip remains etched in my mind as a huge success and formative experience for me personally and professionally.

As it happened, my new Swiss and Dutch friends didn't give up and became my biggest sales and promotion teams. That trip was just the beginning!

VENTURING FARTHER EAST

Before I describe Siegfried's entry into the relatively difficult Japanese market, I'd like to offer some background on Japanese and Taiwanese relationships.

For fifty years, from 1895 to 1945, Taiwan was occupied by Japan. Then, it returned to Chinese control, and, frankly, our two countries share a dislike for Mainland China. If China were to make good on its threats to attack Taiwan, Japan would become involved to protect Taiwan at all costs.

Thus, Taiwan and Japan are closely allied geopolitically—we protect each other from political enemies and natural disasters. A striking example followed the magnitude 9.0 earthquake and tsunami that ravaged Japan in March 2011. The Fukushima Daiichi reactors went down, becoming the biggest nuclear disaster since the 1986 Chernobyl meltdown. Taiwan, a small country of twenty-three million people, put together the largest donation of any place worldwide for relief efforts and sent teams to search for survivors.

The pre-WWII occupation of Taiwan by Japan blended our cultures. It taught us how to conduct ourselves carefully, delicately, and respectfully. This still holds true today in business and in personal relationships. It has contributed to Taiwan's ability to manufacture semiconductor chips, which are extremely fragile microelectronics, better than anywhere else in the world.

Japanese people are known for their hardworking ethic. There's a joke that if a man comes home at 9:00 p.m., his wife considers him lazy. But it's not a joke. There's a well-documented tragic phenomenon called *karoshi*, death by overwork, that has plagued Japanese society. However, many of the Japanese people I deal with are US-educated, and I haven't come across any unhealthy workaholics.

Both Taiwan and Japan deliver on their promises and deliver them on time, building trust and mutual admiration. People from Hong Kong and those from the West do not understand our closeness. Although Taiwan has three major cultures—Japanese, Chinese, and American—its ties with Japan are strong and enduring. When Taiwanese people travel abroad, 60 percent visit Japan. And in Taiwan, we have the best sushi outside of Japan!

Taiwan and Japan are also friendly baseball competitors. Recently, they played in an international tournament, the Baseball Premium 12, and Taiwan went head-to-head with Japan in the finals. Taiwan won the gold medal, its first in twenty-eight previous major world games.[9] It's a reflection of our closeness that after the game, my Japanese partners immediately emailed me to offer their congratulations.

I recognize that I am generalizing about countries and cultures, but my comments are based on my firsthand experiences, and many others share my views. I recommend Ezra Vogel's 1979 book, *Japan as Number One: Lessons for America*, which documents Japan's social, economic, industrial, educational, and environmental strengths.[10]

GETTING DOWN TO BUSINESS

Japan is a very tough market for businesses to penetrate. The Japanese tend to distrust outsiders and are very conservative. As is my habit, I attribute a lot of my success there to good luck!

People in Taiwan and Hong Kong are amazed to learn that Siegfried has partnered with Japanese investors, particularly since they are super conservative fiscally, preferring safe, small deals.

However, when you agree on the terms of a deal with Japanese businesspeople, you can be assured they will fulfill them. A handshake agreement can be trusted. Also, the Japanese communicate directly to your face, unlike the Chinese (or the Southern Italians I dealt with on solar power plants years ago). It is a pleasure to interact with straightforward, like-minded businesspeople.

As of June 2025, Siegfried has conducted five road shows in Japan. Back in 2021 we established a strong partnership with Bayview Asset Management there. They liked my investment product, as it delivers low-risk, stable income. They told me they wanted to present my company exclusively. I responded with equal directness, asking them about their capacity, as Japan is a huge market. I told them if they invested $500 million, we would consummate the deal. They agreed and won the exclusivity of Siegfried in Japan without hesitation.

When I visit annually, the Japanese introduce me to their many institutional clients—banks, insurance companies, securities companies, etc. My trips usually span four consecutive days with up to twenty-five back-to-back meetings where I repeat the same speech over and over to prospective clients.

I have worked relentlessly in my life and have certainly proven I am undaunted by challenges. When I embark on an adventure, especially in new territory, I am often guided by another favorite maxim—this one from the philosopher Lao Tzu: "千里之行，始于足下," which translates to "A journey of a thousand miles begins with a single step." As you have gathered by now, I intend to keep walking!

11

Siegfried's Secret Sauce: Full Transparency

How do you start a business, any business, when no one knows who you are? How do you start a business when your product, though having demonstrable, positive results, is novel? When it is something based on ideas few people have encountered before? How do you start a business when you are an outsider trying to attract people in a foreign country?

The challenges these questions raise are even more complicated when asking for a financial investment in your company and, by extension, in you. Economic fluctuations and volatility in market competition, currency exchange rates, interest rates, unemployment, regulatory requirements, global political instability, environmental disasters, and much more can all work against you.

Further, these challenges are magnified when you are trying to enter global financial markets. So, how did we overcome these challenges and transform from a struggling modest fund into an international powerhouse—especially in the Japanese and US markets?

Some of my preparation for this feat dates back to 2010, years before I established Siegfried. That's when I added a PhD in economics from Nankai University in Tianjin, China, to my academic credentials. These further studies offered new perspectives on global finance and may have even contributed to my marketability and credibility.

Still, I would say that my hands-on work in business, my stick-to-itiveness, and my resilience paved the way for Siegfried's gradual upward trajectory. Let me show you what I mean.

THE NUMBERS STORY

Siegfried's bottom line may have jumped over six years from $15 million in 2018 to $3.1 billion in 2025, but you will recall that I began developing Siegfried in 2015 and had several disappointing starts. The pilot project, which launched in 2018 with $15 million from friends and family investors, was a small step in the right direction. However, the fund didn't begin to attract substantial institutional investments for several years. It was only after the first banking client invested that others quickly followed.

The $500 million I set as a point of entry before meeting with the good people at Bayview Asset Management was a well-reasoned goal. Siegfried was offering solid, investment-grade account receivables (the business model we discussed earlier as *factoring*) only to institutional investors, such as banks, securities firms, insurance companies, and endowment funds. These are solid prospective clients with experienced professional investors and impressive track records.

Such investors would view any fund with assets under management (AUM) in the range of $300 million as too small to even consider. So, I determined that $500 million would be the sweet spot for Siegfried. It would be a milestone achievement, helping us to overcome significant barriers of entry, not the least of which were fear of risk and fear of the unknown. As I've said before, investors didn't know me or my product and were skeptical about the return on investment I promised.

Although I could prove my factoring model worked and garnered investors' interest, no one wanted to be the first to invest. Everyone wanted to "wait and see."

So, I had to wait, too. But I was certainly not idle; to the contrary, I actively tweaked my business model. I embarked on many "dog and pony shows," traveling to make presentations to everyone I knew and speaking to hundreds of people I did not know—contacts of contacts, and their contacts. I identified additional prospects and attracted their interest. I am grateful to Dr. Typhoon

Wen, Alan Hung, Mr. X, and others who helped me in this process. And I am grateful to Bayview Asset Management for taking the bold step to be the first in Japan. Our relationship has been fruitful for both of us.

Throughout this long growth trajectory, I had no intention of giving up! According to another Chinese saying, "不怕慢，就怕站," which means, "It does not matter how slowly you go so long as you do not stop." I did not halt; I moved forward step-by-step until I found my way.

Some of the investment deals Siegfried made involved projects that took a year or more to come to fruition. We purposely began with only seven employees, so the business could remain sustainable. We could feed everybody, including my family—no small achievement for someone still paying down a $10 million debt I did not personally incur, a debt that I am glad to say has *finally* been discharged. Whatever the obstacles, I remained undeterred.

THE RED FLAG . . . OF FORTUNE!

I mentioned earlier that 2021 was a pivotal year. Even before doing business with Bayview, I was negotiating with an institutional fund in London that seemed poised to make our first big-ticket investment: $80 million. But something inexplicable held them back. Even after we offered full transparency and assuaged their doubts, they still hesitated.

I am not superstitious; I am a conservative, rational financial engineer. I don't believe in mysterious forces that can change the course of events. However, in February 2021, on the third (and last) day of the Chinese New Year celebration, I received a good omen. Tradition says that the gods of fortune visit that day, and everyone lines up when they get home to receive a red envelope for good luck.

When it was my turn in line, the doorman told me, "Today is your lucky day!" Instead of receiving a red envelope like everyone else, I received a red flag. This symbolized a potential for the best luck of all. It was like winning the lottery.

The red flag meant "go, go, go, you can win." It is the polar opposite of a red light warning you to stop.

I hung the flag in front of my house, and, lo and behold, Siegfried got an order from the London-based asset manager within a few days! This was a huge turning point for the fund and my life. Maybe the deal's timing wasn't the work of the gods; maybe, since I am not superstitious, it was the result of human effort; or maybe it was just coincidental. Regardless, I was blessed.

It is traditional to take the red flag down after the Chinese New Year, but I kept it in front of my house for eight months until it became worn out and dirty. My good fortune remained, as we continued to receive large orders from Japan in that same year.

HARD WORK BROUGHT MORE GOOD FORTUNE

It may seem surprising, but a significant increase in our revenues occurred during the COVID-19 pandemic. We began having good results in Europe in February 2020. As I described, my receiving the red flag preceded our big breakthrough in London in February 2021 and Japan in July 2021.

By the end of 2021, Siegfried's $200 million in AUM had jumped up to $1 billion; in 2022, we hit $2.2 billion; and in 2023, we broke through in US markets, which predictably wasn't easy. US institutional investors tend to be speculators looking for double-digit returns. However, we convinced them that we could deliver a *stable* return of 8 to 10 percent, and they bought into the fund's reliability and sustainability.

Nevertheless, the path to hitting these numbers wasn't always smooth. In 2022, the Japanese yen (JPY) and the US dollar (USD) currency exchange ratio was low—USD 1 to JPY 114. However, the yen declined significantly after a year and a half, and the exchange ratio changed from USD 1 to JPY 161.

This decline presented a significant problem for Siegfried because we had to hedge our Japanese yen from investors' subscriptions to our USD investments.

Before the yen's value declined against the dollar, the hedging cost was at 2 percent; at its worst, it was as high as 7 percent.

Of course, the 7 percent cost impacted our JPY class return—our returns were still good but only slightly better than Japanese bond yields because we relied on hedging our trades. We explained to our clients that this was a macro, not a micro, financial problem; fortunately, they waited it out. The wait was worthwhile; the result turned out to be satisfactory.

Siegfried took off! As I said, no one wanted to be the first to come on board. But everyone started to follow once we had these solid cornerstone investments from large international banks. In 2025, we reached $3.1 billion in AUM, far exceeding my initial hopes. The financial world took notice, too.

OPENING THE BOOKS

Let's get back to the questions I raised at the beginning of this chapter: Why would a professional investor choose to do business with me and my company, an unknown entity from a foreign country with a novel financial model? How did Siegfried differentiate itself from other hedge funds? How did Siegfried get this far? I can answer these questions in one word: *transparency*.

I completely opened the company's books and records for anyone to see. Siegfried's inner workings and all its financial data were available for scrutiny. When savvy professional investors did their due diligence, the information they requested was accessible and transparent. And best of all, they liked what they saw; I hid nothing.

Prospects could examine all the financial metrics that determine the bottom line: the track records, transaction documents, all fees and expenses, income rates, projections, and more. As I said, I hid nothing.

Business relationships rely on trust. So, when institutional investors ask us anything, they get an honest answer. They ask about my employees' salaries to determine if Siegfried's operations are stable. They ask about my personal compensation package to judge how I allocate the company's resources, and, most importantly, to assess my character. We also have an open-book management policy, enabling employees to access the fund's financial records; I still hide nothing.

Siegfried continues to operate with full transparency. I also manage my personal life and finances openly and honestly, as I hope I've demonstrated throughout this book. I am a man of integrity.

There are two significant benefits to being open: First, people appreciate your candor, and second, they like what they see. Additionally, I am confident in what we offer: select, investment-grade quality receivables from large companies with strong credit ratings. Psychologically, banks are buying assets directly rather than investing in Siegfried's fund. Further, since account receivables are like loans, banks can book them as assets on their own balance sheets.

Maybe well-known heavy hitters like Blackstone, Carlyle, KKR, or Millenium can still get by on their reputations. Investors are usually happy when they see growth in their bank accounts or receive checks in the mail, so they don't look too closely. But as an unknown, Siegfried takes a different approach: We make ourselves known down to the penny. We are proud to demonstrate our inner workings and financials.

Some businesses want to keep their books closed because they think they have "trade secrets" and fear companies will copy their business model. However, people became more cautious after Bernie Madoff's massive Ponzi scheme was uncovered in the early 2000s. He was found guilty of defrauding banks, universities, charitable foundations, retirement plans, and individuals, and they all lost billions. Investors lost trust and became more cautious.[11]

I recently spoke to a large Japanese securities firm. They said they had been monitoring Siegfried for several years. They had spoken to other fund managers with similar products, but I was the only one who offered complete transparency, and they greatly appreciated that.

I'm often asked by investors how big Siegfried intends to grow. Global trade is around $3 trillion per annum, and global trade associated with the Asian market is around $1.5 trillion annually. Since we only focus on the investment-grade quality of the buyers' purchases, I estimate the capacity for what we can do is around $20 billion or more. But I think I am happy with a cap of $10 billion.

I'm already happy with our current size of $3 billion and growing, but we could easily manage to quadruple our AUM someday. I don't lack prospects; I can tap a steady pipeline of institutional investors. But I'm not hurrying to make new deals. We can afford to be selective. I don't want Siegfried to get so big that it hurts our track record of returns (as it did at one point to Fidelity and the Magellan Fund). I'm in no rush; I am confident Siegfried will grow methodically and organically.

ANOTHER SECRET INGREDIENT: RESILIENCE

As someone who was, at best, ignored as a kid and, at worst, belittled, I must admit that my personal growth and character have contributed to my success. This confidence was hard-won.

As you know from earlier chapters, I always read voraciously, and in college, I studied hard. But the real key was that I stayed very focused. I can automatically filter out the noise of people around me offering opinions on the financial markets. I trust my own thinking and believe in what I do. I don't deviate from my path.

When I studied in Wichita and New York, I lived alone in small apartments filled with books. I always relished my solitude and time for introspection. I would happily go to movies and restaurants and travel alone.

I mentioned earlier that I admire Warren Buffett and have read a lot about him. He gave a compelling reason for why he lived in Omaha, Nebraska, instead of a big city like New York or San Francisco. Buffett said that he didn't want to make any momentous decisions amid the hubbub and noise of a big city. He needed peace and quiet to think carefully and analyze deeply.

Even though I live in Taiwan and Hong Kong and do business in major metropolitan centers worldwide, I still have an innate ability to shut out distractions. I remain centered and humbled. My concentration, effort, and diligence have been rewarded. But I will never forget the red flag of good fortune.

12

Gamification: Getting to the Next Level

Although the financial world considers Siegfried a hedge fund, our investment strategy is closer to that of a money market or a cash alternative instrument. A typical hedge fund might boast high returns, but their investments come with higher risks because they are subject to the whims of the market's volatility.

In contrast, Siegfried's rate of return is steady at approximately 8 to 10 percent a year. That rate may be lower than the one-year return of another fund, but it's certainly not nothing, and it's reliably repeatable. Ten percent is a phenomenal result compared to a traditional savings account in the US, earning under 4 percent in early 2025! In previous chapters, I've detailed our strategy and yields, but you'll soon see why it bears mentioning again here. (Hint: It has resulted in financial industry recognition.)

Hedge funds use a measurement calculation called the Sharpe ratio, which compares the investment return over risk-free rates (often referred to as the three-month US treasury bill yield) to its performance risk (often referred to as the standard deviation of performance). We understand this concept, as do institutional investors; consequently, we capture their interest (pun intended).

Siegfried's strategic calculations have yielded positive results for our existing investors and enabled us to penetrate new markets in Europe, Japan, and the US successfully. In 2024, Siegfried was in an enviable financial position, and the industry took notice.

FINANCIAL INDUSTRY AWARDS

When the financial industry honors a company for its performance, it uses the adjusted risk ratio, not just the company's calculations. A "best hedge fund" award is particularly meaningful when Hedge Fund Managers (HFM)—a global hedge fund database under With Intelligence, or Bloomberg, an internationally respected financial, trading platform, and media company—bestow the honor.

Despite our different investment strategies, HFM and Bloomberg define Siegfried as a hedge fund. When I taught financial engineering at university, I would tell students that there were eleven hedge fund strategies. Now, I joke that there are more than fifty! When we are selected as winners in the same categories as other hedge funds, it is understood that the award grantors use the risk-adjusted return calculation.

In November 2022, Siegfried won the Best Performing Asian Hedge Fund Award by HFM in the Specialty Credit and Finance subcategory. This was our first significant award, and it was thrilling. The awards ceremony was held in Singapore, and it felt like attending the Oscars. For each category, the nominees were listed on a screen, and then the presenter opened an envelope and announced, "And the winner is . . ." The Siegfried team was shocked and ecstatic to hear our company's name. When I was ushered to the stage to receive the prestigious trophy, I couldn't help but think how far I'd come since the time my moniker was "Mr. 2.7."

The same year, 2022, Siegfried won the Best Performing Emerging Hedge Fund Award by *Bloomberg Businessweek*. It was awesome to be considered the best. Whereas the financial services industry looks to the HFM awards, the Bloomberg awards are more meaningful to the public. I am happy to be recognized in both circles!

In 2023, the HFM categories changed. Although we were nominated for Best Performance for Credit and Special Finance, we did not win. The following year, the

HFM categories changed again, and we were nominated in the big category of Fixed Income. That put us in the shark tank with all the big players in the market. We missed out on winning again.

I was still thrilled. As I've said, I call myself Silver because I don't have to be gold to shine. Being nominated is already an honor, and it has been good enough for me! There are so many hedge funds and so many smart, business-savvy people out there that a win is a win.

In 2024, Siegfried won Bloomberg's most prestigious award: Best Performing Hedge Fund over $500 million AUM. This is a particularly significant award as it is not a sub-category award. We'd made it to the top after competing with all the big players with AUM over $500 million, a feat in and of itself, and Bloomberg's award was icing on the cake. It was also a tremendous morale booster for my team—they are happy, I am happy, and our investors are happy. The bottom line is that when our investors are happy, they will not only stay with us, they will also consider adding more capital to the fund. Further, our business partners in Europe, Japan, and the US can use this news in a marketing campaign.

Bloomberg Businessweek published an article about the award in their weekly magazine, including a two-page spread about our company's story. I was interviewed for the article, and the ceremony was held in Hong Kong in March 2025. What a tremendous feeling to hold a trophy and have cameras flashing and people clapping!

The excitement was contagious even for a calm, rational guy like me.

Siegfried hosted a private party for our entire team with a live band, a famous singer, free-flowing liquor—it was wild! As I've said, I've been happy with Siegfried's performance and growth, but self-congratulation differs from recognition by a well-known, respected global leader like Bloomberg. I am very happy and grateful to our team members. Of course, from a business perspective, awards like this go a long way toward retaining investors and gaining new ones.

A VIDEO GAME MENTALITY

How do I feel about the tremendous growth of my personal wealth? Honestly, I don't feel much. At the risk of sounding flippant, having $100 million for me is the same as having $5 million. As I've said, I don't spend a lot of money; I certainly don't spend as extravagantly as my means would allow. Yes, nice hotels and parties are fun, but I've never cared much about material things. Remember that as a young man, I never had money, and so I learned to live frugally.

I view the upward trajectory of Siegfried and my personal profits as a video game. Don't get me wrong; I don't mean it's child's play or insignificant. Instead, it's like conquering the game's quests, getting to the next level, and stacking up higher and higher scores. Every day as

I do something right, my score increases. As I climb, I receive additional tools and new skills to fuel my success, so winning breeds more winning. (By the way, many academic studies have demonstrated that elements of video gaming, especially its built-in motivational incentives, significantly impact learning and promote mastery.)

My motivation for playing is to continually break my own records. Best of all, I'm having fun every step of the journey. As a lifelong learner, the intrinsic rewards I derive from Siegfried hitting new targets or financial "levels" are as significant, if not more so, than the extrinsic awards and accolades we've earned.

I don't envision the game ever ending, because I can't stay put! It's fun when a business is stable, but I always have new pursuits. There are always new projects and ideas, new people to meet, and new places to see. I've always been eager to learn, and there are always new mountains of knowledge to climb. I constantly seek new quests, like making deals with investors who are difficult to approach or penetrating untapped markets.

Traveling and exposure to new scenery and different cultures (and food and wine!) provide a fascinating learning opportunity for me and my family. Even without money, I would figure out ways to fund my travel. You might remember how I tripled my parents' $8,000 graduate-school tuition contribution by setting up an E*TRADE account and how I used the proceeds to travel through Europe.

Today, I use my "winnings" from much more significant investments to travel all over the world. I recently had three opportunities to visit India in six months' time. Doriya and I were guests at an incredible five-day Indian wedding. As I mentioned in chapter 10, we were also fortunate to be invited to the Dalai Lama's ninetieth birthday celebration in northern India. Although the celebration was cancelled due to His Holiness's health, we still made the trip and were spiritually uplifted by it. Lastly, I visited Bangalore, the Silicon Valley of India, where I was admittedly challenged to figure out how their Uber system works, as it is very different from what I am familiar with. As Shakespeare wrote, "The world's mine oyster,"[12] and I love shucking open the shells.

After the many twists and turns in my path and the glorious travels I've taken to engage my curiosity, I must say one of the high points in my journey was when I was invited to join R360 Global, one of the most exclusive clubs in the world. For me, accepting that invitation felt as if I'd finished all the quests of the game and broken all the levels and high-score records. Now I can say to myself in the middle of the night: *I made it.*

FAMILY IS THE ULTIMATE LEVEL

Now that I have become financially successful—by some standards, winning the gold instead of the silver medal—I am spending a lot of time and energy building a sustainable, long-term, stable family portfolio for DCIS Trust and family office. Maybe you can guess the origin of the trust's name. (It's the first initials of Doriya, Celine, Irene, and Silver.) My close, personal relationships with the bankers and our mutual respect are going a long way toward making the plans happen.

I am determined to leave a legacy of generational wealth, a far cry from the generational debt I inherited. That is the ultimate game level!

13

The Arts: My Inspiration in Good Times and in Bad

In addition to gaming, my love of the arts—literature, theater, movies, classical music, opera, and ballet—has sustained me over the years. This cultural appreciation was absent from my parents' lives; instead, I discovered the pleasure of the arts on my own. I had promised earlier to share some of the plays, books, and movies that have most inspired and influenced me, so perhaps they may do the same for you. The following provides a deeper explanation of my regard for certain works I've already noted, as well as some works I have not yet mentioned.

It was during my school days in the US that theater and concerts became pleasant diversions and friendly companions. I was resourceful and became adept at finding cheap ways to attend performances, particularly while studying at Pace in New York City. The variety and availability of shows to attend multiplied exponentially there. As I've described, I would spend what little money I had buying cheap, same-day theater tickets at the TKTS booth in Times Square. I saw so many wonderful Broadway musicals, comedies, and dramas that way. I went to concerts at Lincoln Center and saw art films and independent and foreign movies at the iconic Paris Theater nearby. I also went to the Metropolitan Museum of Art and the Metropolitan Opera.

WHY *LES MISÉRABLES*?

You already know that I am a huge *Les Mis* fan. I attended a road company's performance of *Les Misérables* in Wichita and fell head over heels in love with the play—intellectually, artistically, and emotionally. Each subsequent time I see the show, new meanings emerge. As a history fan, I am fascinated with the show's depiction of the French Revolution, particularly its portrayal of the inequities that spawned an underworld economy. The play's appeal for me is also deeply visceral and emotional: I empathize with the downtrodden characters, particularly Fantine. Her circumstances left her impoverished, helpless, and unable to care for her young daughter, Cosette. Her plight reminded me of the dark times when

I was too broke to feed my family. Fantine's despair is all too familiar. Still, *Les Misérables*'s message of hope and resilience prevails.

THE MATRIX

As I described in chapter 6, Doriya Li says she fell in love with me on our first date as I shared my interpretation of *The Matrix*'s deep existential and Zen meanings. How could I not include this movie as one of my all-time favorites?! But I also include it here for another reason: The beauty of the arts for me lies in the freedom of interpretation. With my broad base and analytical mind, I find multilayered meanings in *many* books and movies. (This one just happens to be the epitome of layered works.) Doriya and I have consciously exposed our daughters to the arts since they were young to engage them and open their minds. Not only do they share our appreciation, but they share their thoughts, insights, and interpretations, too. What's more, they are also talented singers and dancers.

THE *BEFORE* TRILOGY

This tender movie trilogy directed, produced, and written by Richard Linklater also ranks high on my list of favorites. It consists of *Before Sunrise* (1995), *Before*

Sunset (2004), and *Before Midnight* (2013). The films feature only two characters—Jesse, played by Ethan Hawke; and Celine, played by Julie Delpy—and follows their romance over eighteen years.

The trilogy portrays the significant stages of the couple's relationship from their first chance encounter to their romance, long-distance relationship, and diverging paths. Each film is made up of intense conversations between the couple. It stimulated my thinking about my own relationships, family, and marriage. Each time I see these films, I gain a new perspective.

The trilogy also realistically presents the dualities of life: hope and disappointment, happiness and sadness, closeness and distance, etc., which we have all experienced. They're a part of the human condition.

WALL STREET: THE 1987 MOVIE

Every year, when I taught investment banking classes at the National Kaohsiung University of Science and Technology, I devoted a class to watching the movie *Wall Street* (1987).[13] Then, I assigned the students to write a paper about it.

Wall Street inspired me to create the road map for my future fund management ventures. Here are some of the quotes that most impacted me, followed by my takeaways:

- "Man looks in the abyss, there's nothing staring back at him. At that moment, man finds his character. And that is what keeps him out of the abyss."

  This thought pulled me out of my own abyss in my darkest days as a young man.

- "Money's only something you need in case you don't die tomorrow . . ."

  This comment keeps me sane and centered while pursuing success.

- "I don't throw darts at a board. I bet on sure things."

  This reminds me of Sun Tzu's *The Art of War*, where he says every battle is won before it is ever fought. I always try to think many steps ahead.

- "Kid, you're on a roll. Enjoy it while it lasts, 'cause it never does."

  I remind myself to take breaks, especially if I am moving too fast, and appreciate what I have.

- "If you're not inside, you're outside!"

  Whatever I do, I try to be *in* the game, in control, or at least be influential.

I hope that my students found meaning in the story and messages of *Wall Street* as well.

A GOOD BOOK IS A GOOD FRIEND

In earlier chapters, I have discussed the solitary lifestyle I chose in undergraduate and graduate school. However, it is worth reiterating that I have always been a reader, from the days of hiding books from my father to the times of reading books at stoplights. I've enjoyed all genres, particularly Chinese history, Greek and Roman mythology, business philosophy, and literature.

In high school, I read *The Romance of the Three Kingdoms*, a historical novel about events in China from 184 to 280 CE by Luo Guanzhong.[14] It is set during the Han dynasty and dramatizes the intrigue between warring factions. I read this seven-hundred-page book more than fifteen times! Each time, it gave me new insights and perspectives on strategic planning. I was similarly fascinated with *The Art of War,* purportedly written in the fifth century BCE by Sun-Tzu.

During my time at Wichita State University, my favorite author was the Japanese writer Haruki Murakami. His first book, *Hear the Wind Sing,* is about a Japanese college student returning home for summer vacation.[15] The book resonated with me as a young loner prone to contemplation and self-examination.

I've already described some of my favorite business books—*The Warren Buffett Way* by Robert G. Hagstrom,[16] which describes Buffett's basic principles; and *The Adventure Capitalist* by Jim Rogers,[17] which recounts his worldwide travels to understand the economics of each region. These are just a few examples of fiction and nonfiction books that have deeply influenced me both personally and professionally.

I love everything about history. I read all kinds of history books pertaining to either Eastern or Western cultures. I have a dream that one day I will have the time and resources to locate where the Lost City of Atlantis is. I often consider myself very much like the ancient Greek hero Odysseus, who is very well described in the book *The Odyssey* by Homer. I feel as if all my life I have been longing to come home, wherever that is, yet I have faced monsters and gone through all kinds of obstacles to do that, as Odysseus did.

I have similar feelings about Siegfried, whom I named my company after. It is a reference from one of my favorite operas, *Der Ring des Nibelungen*, written and composed by Richard Wagner. Wagner spent all of his life on this masterpiece. This opera is really too long for anyone to sit down in the theater and see it all the way through. It takes four days to finish the complete set. All my hero, Siegfried, wanted was a peaceful life with his loved ones, yet he had to go through all the adventures and winding plots to slay the dragon before he could do so.

As you can tell, I love reading. When I was young and alone, I would sometimes randomly open a page of the *Britannica Encyclopedia*. Each item would expand into many other related topics, and I'd be motivated to read further. I would sit there for hours, delving deeper into the layers and layers of topics. I'd lose track of time. I was afloat in the ocean of knowledge, experiencing my type of peace and joy. I still do this today, only now I turn to the internet, specifically to Wikipedia; I could sit down all day and do nothing but read article after article. I sometimes help to edit the entries, too.

When I was in elementary school, we had a wall of books at home belonging to my parents. I tried to read them all. I fell in love with *Reader's Digest*, a subscription magazine my mother received for years. It was not common for younger people in Taiwan to have access to that magazine. Every week, I waited for the postman to deliver it. Sadly, this stopped when I was sent to boarding school at age twelve.

Sometimes I describe myself using the words of a very old Chinese poet, Tao Yuanming, who said, "吾好讀書，不求甚解." This means, "He loves reading but he doesn't have to understand everything." I tend to read fast, and that is how I read a lot. I don't have to remember everything in a book. If there are a few key concepts that I remember and learn from, I will call that book a winner. If I find it interesting or if there are some ideas that puzzle me, I will go back to reread it again and again.

EVERY DAY = MULTIPLE FRACTIONS OF USABLE TIME

How do I find the time to read and go to movies today, as I am busy with a demanding business involving deal-making, attending meetings, reading reports and analyses, traveling all over the world, and caring for my family? My schedule may seem head-spinning, but it isn't overwhelming to me. I still find time to read three to five books and watch five to seven movies every week!

My secret? I make use of every fraction of time available. I believe that our days—yours and mine—consist of segments of seconds, minutes, hours, etc., and they offer the space to do the things that give us pleasure.

Here's an example: When I was twenty years younger, I read a six-volume collection of books by the Chinese author Jin Yong while driving—actual books, not audiobooks. I wouldn't recommend doing that today, as it's not the safest idea, but back then I figured there are sixty seconds of waiting time at each red light, during which I can read two or three pages. And if traffic was slow, I could read even more. Over the course of a few months, I was able to finish a book this way.

Of course, I travel a lot and take increments of time to read books and watch movies while waiting in airports, sitting on airplanes, and waiting for appointments, too. There's a lot of time you can accumulate and use productively. It's up to us not to waste the precious moments we have.

A proverb attributed to Lu Xun, a Chinese writer, illustrates my point about the availability of time: "時間就像海綿裡的水，只要願擠，總還是有的," meaning, "Time is like water in a sponge; as long as you are willing to squeeze, there will always be some."

I find that this is especially true with regard to classical music; I always carve out time to listen to the composers I love—Austrian composer Franz Shubert; Russian composers Tchaikovsky and Rachmaninov; and Italian Baroque composer Vivaldi. I listen to music while I'm walking and while I'm working. When I travel, I arrange my schedule to fit in cultural performances. I also make a point of bringing my girls to concerts. Recently, I traveled with Celine to Budapest, and then we took the train to Prague and Vienna to attend several concerts.

When I have classical music in the background, the music fades, and I become very focused, seeing things more clearly and solving problems. My experience is supported by research. A study published in the journal *Brain Sciences* claims that "music listening improves cognitive functions such as memory, attention span, and behavioral augmentation."[18]

In Hong Kong and Taiwan, I am one of the very few people I know who love this kind of Western culture, especially among those in finance. The vast majority prefer pop music.

CHOOSING MOMENTS AND MEMORIES

Everyone chooses to spend their time and money in different ways. I choose to spend each fraction of my time productively. I choose to spend my money on experiences that provide lasting memories. The arts greatly contribute to those experiences.

Previously, I had hopes and dreams that were denied to me. But through persistence and resilience, I've reached a stage in life where I've achieved success; I am confident that whatever new hopes I have will be attainable! I am very grateful to have many wonderful choices available to me and many new rewarding experiences in wait. Reading all about how far I've come, and how I've done it, you may be a bit curious as to how I envision my future. If so, read on.

14

Final Reflections: Global Citizenry

According to an ancient Chinese proverb, "前人栽樹，後人乘涼," one generation plants the trees, and the next enjoys the shade. This image resonates as I reflect on my life and look toward the future. I will consider myself successful if my family, heirs, and fellow citizens of the world are shielded in comfort from the harsh elements.

My ideas about what happens next are still percolating, but my priorities are legacy planning and philanthropy, including championing climate action.

My next steps for Siegfried Capital are also still brewing. I am comfortable with our size and scale, although I said the same thing two years ago, and we continued to grow. Our partners and investors would like the fund to grow even further, and I feel a responsibility toward them. Still, I've begun to think about my exit strategy.

I considered taking Siegfried public. However, if I followed through, I would no longer be the company owner; I would just be the manager. Why would I cede my company's control and become subject to the myriad of regulations a public company must comply with? I don't need the headaches and I really don't need the money. These are certainly weighty issues to ponder.

A HEAD START, NOT A HANDOUT

How much money is enough? It's a pertinent question. Doriya and I are quite comfortable. We never sought material gain to support a lavish lifestyle. Luxury cars, jewelry, and designer labels are not important to us. I still wear the same brand of jeans (maybe even the same pair) I wore ten years ago!

That said, we enjoy eating at a nice restaurant with good food and a decent bottle of wine. The only notable difference in our dining experience today is that we read the menu to choose what dishes we will enjoy, not to eliminate all the choices we can't afford.

The same love for travel that led me to twenty-five countries before I turned twenty-five still leads me and my family to explore the world. We travel extensively but not extravagantly. When Celine and Irene were very young, we flew only economy class. As our resources improved, my wife and I flew business class for long flights, but the girls stayed in economy. Under no circumstances would we pay to travel first class.

Similarly, we can afford to stay in nice hotels but opt not to stay at over-the-top fancy places. On a recent trip to New York, I used my accumulated hotel reward points to stay free for two full weeks. Our friends were also in town, staying in a suite at the St. Regis on Fifth Avenue and paying $3,000 per night. Per *night*! Could I have afforded to pay that? Frankly, yes. But that is not how I choose to allocate my resources. To me, that's wasteful.

In addition, we spent so many years struggling that fear of losing what we worked so hard to achieve still nags at the corners of my mind and breeds caution.

Celine and Irene's upbringing has grounded and prevented them from becoming spoiled. They both have the knowledge and skills to be fiscally responsible and are capable of earning their own way and managing their finances wisely. They understand that the family trust isn't an ATM dispenser. If they want or need something, like seed capital for a venture, they must bring a formal business proposal to an independent trustee for consideration.

Of course, I want the girls to have a comfortable life and am pleased to give them a head start, but not a handout. When Celine and Irene graduated from high school and began their studies at NYU, I transferred the ownership of one of our condos to each of them. The units are currently being rented, so Celine and Irene manage the rental, file the required taxes, and do any necessary repairs and maintenance.

They can use the property's income to support themselves. I am paying their university tuitions, but they are responsible for all their living expenses. That's a wonderful head start over their peers.

However, this is very different from giving a big lump sum to your kid in their twenties. With such a gift in hand, human nature tends to remove the motivation to work.

IMPACT INVESTING

I have established a long-term irrevocable dynasty trust, which is designed to survive and provide for generations. It has provisions for using money to pay for university tuition and specified emergencies, but no lump-sum payments or scheduled distributions. I will manage the trust until I decide to hire someone else to manage it under my will.

The name of my family trust, DCIS Capital—which, as I told you earlier, derives from the first letter of each of our four names—says volumes about our family's dynamic; I am very proud of how close the four of us are. This is highly unusual in Taiwanese society, where typically the father is considered the ruling god and communication is limited.

My objectives for the DCIS and Siegfried investment portfolios are twofold: to earn a profit and make lasting impacts on humanity. I am driven by a desire to protect the environment in general, and particularly to clean the ocean. Many areas are clogged with islands of plastic destroying the ecosystem, and I've invested in companies that are developing technologies to address the problem. I also donate to NGOs, including Greenpeace.

I am pleased to support global climate-action initiatives. In 2015, all UN Member States developed seventeen Sustainable Development Goals (SDGs), an ambitious agenda for 2030 aimed at eradicating poverty and hunger, while tackling climate change and working to preserve our oceans and forests. My sustainability priorities are goals thirteen, fourteen, and fifteen on that agenda: climate action, life below water, and life on land.

As a signatory of the United Nations Principles of Responsible Investments (UNPRI), Siegfried pledges that its investments will follow UNPRI's guidance. For example, if a company has strong financial positions but is against PRIs, we do not invest in them. Environmental, social, and governance (ESG) principles are at the core of our business. However, I caution: ESG scores can be misleading. For example, companies like Exxon, Phillips, British Petroleum, and tobacco companies are highly rated but are not environmentally friendly, so we don't invest in them. Allow me to elaborate. Big corporates can pay big bucks to assemble a big independent directors of the board to boost their G (Governance) score and they can also spend a lot of money to charities to lift their S (Social) scores. Despite their E (Environmental) score being low, the added up ESG score is still very high. Hence this is misleading.

SUSTAINABILITY: A COLLECTIVE OF MONEY, MINDS, AND EFFORTS

I overcome the limitations of what I can do as one individual with one company by leveraging the power of the collective to make more of an impact on climate change. Siegfried is a client of UBS in Zurich, Switzerland, and UBS pulled together resources to establish a foundation, the UBS Optimus Foundation, for their investor philanthropists. Celine, Irene, and I joined the foundation and participate in meetings, field trips, and project updates.

Last year, we went together with one of the NGOs to the very poor villages in the Vietnam's Mekong Delta. We witnessed devastating poverty and hunger firsthand. The desperate villagers were cutting down mangrove trees to sell for money to buy food. However, they did not realize the environmental harm they were causing. (When you are starving, global warming isn't first and foremost on your mind.)

Mangroves are hugely important to the environment—they are the lungs of the earth. They absorb more carbon dioxide than any other trees in the world and produce twice as much oxygen as the Amazon rainforest.[19] Starvation was forcing the villagers to destroy them. The NGO organized a team to convince the local government to pay these people as forest rangers—to patrol and protect the mangroves instead of destroying them.

My daughters and I spent time speaking with the villagers and it was an extremely meaningful trip. Moving forward, I want to focus my efforts on this kind of collaborative climate action, not just write a check.

A GLOBAL CITIZEN

I hope that my daughters have learned the fundamental values of human decency and hard work through my example. Most of all, I hope they understand there is always a way forward.

I have come a very long way from rock bottom. From a kid $10 million in debt to a global asset manager. From a student with a 2.7 GPA to a lifelong learner with degrees in aerospace engineering, finance, and economics. The road has taken me across the globe from Taiwan to Wichita to New York to Southern Italy to Luxembourg to Japan and Hong Kong. Along the way, I have been blessed to have Doriya by my side.

I have lived in multiple countries and visited countless others. But this fact alone does not make me a citizen of the world. A global citizen is someone who understands they are part of something larger than themselves and takes an active role in making our planet sustainable, peaceful, and equitable for all. Thus, climate action has become a priority for me.

Again, nothing came easy to me. But I never stopped trying. I always found creative solutions and new opportunities. That resilience and persistence are my most cherished legacy.

I would love nothing more than for my story to fill you with hope—for it to inspire you to move forward with your goals, touching one stone at a time when you venture into unfamiliar waters. And for it to spur you to keep a larger global purpose in mind as you succeed, paying your fortune forward in gratitude.

I wish you the best of luck as you work hard toward achieving this reality.

ACKNOWLEDGMENTS

This book represents the sum of many journeys—across continents, careers, and life stages—and it would not have been possible without the support, guidance, and love of so many people.

First and foremost, I thank my wife, Doriya, whose strength, wisdom, and unwavering belief in me were the anchors through my most uncertain times. You've stood beside me with grace and humor, and I am eternally grateful. To my daughters, Celine and Irene, your light and curiosity give my life meaning and joy beyond words. You are the future I strive for. Having you in my life is the greatest blessing and purest joy I've ever known. Your laughter, questions, and even stubborn moments fill my heart daily—you are my constant encouragement and deepest motivation to keep going, no matter what.

To my extended family, thank you for being part of my story, whether as supporters, challengers, or silent observers. Each interaction shaped my perspective and my path.

To my mentors, colleagues, and partners—especially those who believed in me when I had little more than an idea—your trust allowed me to build something meaningful. I am especially grateful to Dr. Typhoon Wen, Alan Hung, Mr. X, and the early investors in Siegfried Capital who gave me a chance to prove what was possible.

To Charlie Garcia, thank you for welcoming me into the R360 community and encouraging me to share my story. Without your support, this book never would have been written. You helped light the spark.

To Michael Levin, my partner in launching our New York Broadway project, I miss all those thoughtful conversations that helped me organize my memories and ideas. Your encouragement and insight were instrumental in bringing this book to life.

To my editors, especially Hope Innelli, thank you for your patience, precision, and dedication in helping me express myself clearly in a language that is not my mother tongue. Your thoughtful guidance helped me shape this book into something I am truly proud of.

To my publisher, Forefront Books, and especially Kia Harris, thank you for assembling the talented team that helped me step into a space that was entirely unknown to me. Your leadership and belief in this project were crucial in bringing it to fruition.

A special thank-you to the teams at Siegfried who have worked tirelessly and with conviction. This book is not just about one man's journey—it is about what can be achieved when people work together with purpose and integrity.

From the bottom of my heart: *Thank you.*

—Silver Kung

NOTES

1. "Typhoon Kong-rey Hits Taiwan's East Coast, Leaving 2 Dead, Hundreds Injured," AP News, updated October 31, 2024, https://apnews.com/article/asia-typhoon-taiwan-philippines-effcd501d9e665be7a7b093821f0adc3.
2. Robert Daugherty, "This Simple One-Page Method Made Warren Buffett Hundreds of Billions," *Forbes*, May 29, 2025, https://www.forbes.com/sites/robertdaugherty/2025/05/29/this-simple-one-page-method-made-warren-buffett-hundreds-of-billions/.
3. Jim Rogers, *The Adventure Capitalist: The Ultimate Road Trip* (Random House, 2003).
4. "President Truman's Remarks at the Wright Memorial Dinner of the Aero Club," speech, December 17, 1952, Harry S. Truman Library and Museum, https://www.trumanlibrary.gov/soundrecording-records/sr60-133-president-trumans-remarks-wright-memorial-dinner-aero-club.
5. Robert Louis Stevenson, *Treasure Island* (1883; Penguin Clothbound Classics, 2016).

6. Fintech-VTeam Financial Service Group, accessed January 21, 2026, https://www.vteamgroup.com/en/show-6.html?utm_source=chatgpt.com.
7. Mark Jahn, "Which Country Is the Largest Exporter of Goods in the World?" Investopedia, updated November 17, 2024, https://www.investopedia.com/ask/answers/011915/what-country-worlds-largest-exporter-goods.asp#.
8. "Why is Luxembourg Such a Sought-After Destination for Fund Governance?" Ocorian, April 30, 2024, https://www.ocorian.com/knowledge-hub/insights/why-luxembourg-such-sought-after-destination-fund-governance.
9. Michael Clair, "Chinese Taipei Wins Gold in Premier12 with Stunning Upset over Japan," MLB, November 24, 2024, https://www.mlb.com/news/chinese-taipei-wins-first-gold-in-upset-of-japan.
10. Ezra Vogel, *Japan as Number One: Lessons for America* (Harvard University Press, 1979).
11. Diana B. Henriques and Zachery Rouwe, "Bernard L. Madoff: Master of the Ponzi Scheme," *The New York Times*, December 12, 2008, https://graphics8.nytimes.com/packages/other/times-premier/madoff.pdf.
12. William Shakespeare, *The Merry Wives of Windsor*, Act II, Scene 2.
13. Oliver Stone, director, *Wall Street*, 1987, Twentieth Century Fox.
14. "Romance of the Three Kingdoms," Wikipedia, January 15, 2026, https://en.wikipedia.org/wiki/Romance_of_the_Three_Kingdoms.

15. Haruki Murakami, *Hear the Wind Sing* (*Gunzo* literary magazine, 1979).
16. Robert G. Hagstrom, *The Warren Buffett Way*, 3rd ed. (Wiley, 2013).
17. Jim Rogers, *The Adventure Capitalist: The Ultimate Road Trip* (Random House, 2004).
18. Corneliu Toader et al., "Cognitive Crescendo: How Music Shapes the Brain's Structure and Function," *Brain Sciences* 13, no. 10 (2023): 1390, https://doi.org/10.3390/brainsci13101390.
19. Daisy Dunne, "Amazon Mangroves 'Twice as Carbon Rich' as Its Rainforests," *Carbon Brief*, September 5, 2018, https://www.carbonbrief.org/amazon-mangroves-twice-as-carbon-rich-as-its-rainforests/.

ABOUT THE AUTHOR

Dr. Silver Kung is a global investment leader, entrepreneur, and sustainability advocate with more than two decades of experience in capital markets and asset management. As the Founder and Chairman of Siegfried Capital Group and Siegfried Asset Management Limited, he has built a career at the forefront of hedge funds, renewable energy private equity, and trade finance innovation. Today, he serves as Executive Director of a Luxembourg CSSF-regulated SICAV fund and multiple AIF and Cayman funds, guiding institutional investors across the globe through complex, high-impact financial strategies.

Born and raised in Taiwan and educated in the United States and China, Silver holds a B.S. in Aerospace Engineering, an M.S. in Finance, and a Ph.D. in Economics. His early ventures included founding Hyperion Capital Management in 2011, where he led solar investments across Italy and Spain. In 2015, he launched Siegfried Capital to champion the emerging asset class of supply chain finance, now the firm's singular focus.

Silver's leadership is deeply rooted in responsible investing. A member of UBS's Global Philanthropy Climate Change Collective, he has positioned Siegfried Capital as a signatory to the UN Principles for Responsible Investment (UN PRI).

Beyond finance, Silver is a devoted husband to Doriya and proud father to daughters Celine and Irene. He's a passionate traveler, cinephile, and history enthusiast—forever curious and inspired by the world's cultural richness. Whether exploring markets or medieval ruins, Silver Kung brings a relentless spirit of discovery and global perspective to everything he does.